The Deepening Crisis
of U.S. Capitalism

The Deepening Crisis of U.S. Capitalism

by Harry Magdoff and Paul M. Sweezy

Monthly Review Press
New York and London

Library of Congress Cataloging in Publication Data

Magdoff, Harry.
  The deepening crisis of U.S. capitalism.

  Includes bibliographical references.
    1. United States—Economic conditions—1971–
2. Capitalism.   I. Sweezy, Paul Marlor, 1910-
II. Title.
HC106.7.M299   330.973'0927   80-8935
ISBN 0-85345-573-2   AACR2
ISBN 0-85345-574-0 (pbk.)

Manufactured in the United States of America

10 9 8 7 6 5 4 3 2

Contents

Introduction

There was a time not so long ago when only radical critics talked about the long wave of post-Second World War prosperity coming to an end. The business and financial community and its experts could see only endless prosperity, at the very least a continuation of the trends established in the twenty-five years between 1945 and 1970, interrupted on occasion by minor recessions. In fact, in the very years when signs of the waning of prosperity abounded, orthodox economists kept on boasting about the power of their New Economics, assisted by elaborate econometric models and some ideas borrowed from Keynes, to keep business rollicking along. A prize example of this confident crowing is a statement made toward the end of 1968 by Professor Paul Samuelson, the first Nobel laureate in economics:

> Our economic system has far surpassed the prophecies of even the most optimistic experts. *The New Economics really does work.* Wall Street knows it. Main Street, which has been enjoying 92 months of advancing sales, knows it. The accountants who chalk up record corporate profits know it . . . and so do the school nurses who measure the heights and weights of this generation and remember the bony structure of the last. You can bet the statisticians of the Kremlin know it—down to the last hundred million of GNP.
>
> Who does not know it? Of course, the exponents of orthodox finance deny the obvious. . . . And how could the New Left forget what it has never learned, or wanted to know?*

---

*Newsweek, November 4, 1968, as quoted in Richard B. DuBoff and Edward S. Herman, "The New Economics: Handmaiden of Inspired Truth," *The Review of Radical Political Economics,* August 1972.

This was written when U.S. involvement in the Vietnamese war was expanding, the ballooning of the fragile debt-prop to business was well under way, and inflation had begun its spiral into the stratosphere. Only two years later, the financial markets barely escaped a threatening crisis, and by early 1971 the United States was forced to renege on its commitment under an international treaty to convert foreign-held dollars to gold, and the dollar had to be devalued twice in rapid succession. These events were followed by twenty-seven bank failures from 1974 to 1976, including two banks with assets of over a billion dollars (the U.S. National Bank of San Diego in 1973 and the Franklin National Bank of New York in 1974). Main Street soon became aware that a new era was looming: A high and rising rate of unemployment persisted throughout the 1970s; and business failures, as measured by liabilities, more than doubled in the 1970s as compared with the 1960s.

Based on this bitter experience, Wall Street too had to change its mind about the magic of the New Economics. Henry Kaufman, partner and member of the executive committee of Salomon Brothers (one of the largest and most influential firms in the New York money market) summarized the change in perspective as follows:

> It seemed that modern economics had found ways to prevent the crises and panics that had hit most earlier generations at least once in their lifetime. There was much that was reassuring besides the reasonable economic performance of the 1950s and early 1960s. The monitoring of economics and finance intensified with the frequent collection of many new data. The advent of econometrics held forth great promise of expanding our understanding of economic behavior. Even the language of economists contained great assurance. More economists spoke convincingly about objectives and made bold predictions about future stability.
>
> When a financial crisis finally struck it was not the old-fashioned kind. It was rather mild. It was called the credit crunch of 1966. "Crunch" was too harsh a label, but like any crisis it was a surprise to the postwar generation, and for a while it laid siege to the savings deposit institutions. The subsequent crises, however, were of increasing intensity. During their most intensive moments, they contained all the ingredients that had fueled the financial debacles of old. How close we came to disaster in 1970, and then again in 1974

and early 1975, no one will ever accurately record. It was a frightening period with rapidly rising interest rates, some spectacular business failures, spiralling preferences for high credit quality and liquidity, and doubts about the strength of some of the largest and most prominent financial institutions.*

Although Kaufman was one of the first to speak openly about financial instability as more than a passing episode, he was soon joined by others. By the time the 1980s dawned, it was no longer the radical critics but important sectors of the business community that became increasingly aware that capitalism was in trouble. "Capitalism Under Stress" was the way the January 1981 issue of *Euromoney* (a journal for international money market operators) headlined its editorial dealing with the problems ahead for the banks involved in lending to the Third World. The former chairman of President Ford's Council of Economic Advisers, Alan Greenspan, entitled his article on the emerging state of affairs in the United States "The Great Malaise" (*Challenge,* March–April 1980). And the winter 1980 enlarged issue of the prestigious *Foreign Affairs* carried an article by two vice presidents of Citibank (Harold van B. Cleveland and Ramachandra Bhagavatula) on "The Continuing World Economic Crisis."

The reason for this marked departure from the earlier optimism and self-confidence is not hard to find. After the experience of the 1970s and the early 1980s,† only the blind or those

---

*Henry Kaufman, "Foreword" to Edward I. Altman and Arnold W. Sametz, *Financial Crises, Institutions and Markets in a Fragile Environment* (New York: John Wiley & Sons, 1977), p. vii.

†In addition to continued volatility in international foreign exchange and commodity markets and the impact of the 1980 recession in the United States on unemployment, business bankruptcies, and chaos in the auto industry, there was the near-collapse of the First Pennsylvania Bank, the largest bank in Philadelphia and the twenty-third largest in the United States. It took a rescue package of $1.5 billion, advanced in April 1980 by the Federal Deposit Insurance Corporation and a group of twenty-two banks, on top of a $700-million loan from the Federal Reserve Bank, to forestall bankruptcy. At about the same time another major rescue operation was under way. Several banks, led by Morgan Guaranty and First National of Dallas, put together a $1-billion loan package as a lifeline to Nelson Bunker Hunt, whose inability to cover enormous losses in the silver futures market was threatening the viability of banks here and abroad that had financed his and his brother's speculations.

who refuse to see could avoid being aware of the fragile nature of the capitalist world's financial fabric. Serious observers of and participants in economic affairs were no longer able to ignore the dangers inherent in the large and growing overhang of dollars outside the United States; the expanding debt load, domestic and foreign; gyrating interest rates; the upsurge in speculation; and the seemingly endless inflation.

But it was not merely the emergence of these problem areas that changed the mood of the business world. There were two other important considerations. First, it became increasingly clear that the various trouble spots were not isolated phenomena. Rather, they were interlinked: intensification of difficulties in one area created strains in others. Second, it became increasingly evident that there was no way to extricate the economy once and for all from its web of financial strains. Each step taken by governments or central banks to avoid disaster induced a further expansion of debt and spurred still more inflation, thus laying the groundwork for a renewal of difficulties in the period to follow.

It is important to understand that the causes of the increasing money market fragility are only partially to be found in the financial system itself: the real root of the problem lies in the continuing stagnation in production and accumulation. Being capitalist institutions, banks and other financial firms operate under the same growth imperatives as do industrial corporations. They are spurred on by competition and the drive to enlarge the profit base. Since the commodity they deal in is money, the key to growth and higher profit lies in marketing an ever growing volume of debt. In and of itself, this is not necessarily dangerous so long as production and the accumulation of capital continue advancing at a sufficiently brisk pace. If this condition is satisfied, increased debt loads can be safely carried, since the payments neccesary to service business and consumer loans can come out of increasing profits and larger personal incomes.

But what happens when production and investment slow down? It is then that the specter of bankruptcy looms in the industrial and financial worlds. The path of least resistance and the first line of defense is to postpone the impending disaster by piling up still more debt to keep the wheels of industry spinning. The banks fit into such a scheme neatly. The ever mounting debt is a source of profit for them, and the maintenance of an increasing flow of funds throughout the economy is needed to save their own necks. All of this, of course, contributes to the intensification of inflation. Inflation, which enables borrowers to sustain debt by repaying with cheaper dollars, in turn becomes essential to keep the whole system afloat. In such an inflationary environment, and in the absence of attractive investment opportunities in expanding the country's underlying industrial capacity, corporations and wealthy individuals increasingly turn to speculation as the way to increase their profits—and they find that the financial community is more than ready to supply new instruments and channels for their swelling speculative activities.

Unrelenting expansion of debt has led to recurrent outbursts of financial instability, but it is important not to lose sight of the fact that in the final analysis the root cause of the trouble has been continuing stagnation in the processes of production and real capital formation. And it is equally important to keep in mind that this particular form of economic illness, far from being confined to the United States, has infected the whole advanced capitalist world during the decade of the 1970s.

Changing patterns of economic growth trends in the United States, Japan, United Kingdom, West Germany, France, and Italy are depicted in the accompanying charts. The solid line in each case shows changes in the index of industrial production from year to year, while the dashed line represents and extends the rate of growth of industrial production during the 1960s. The difference between the solid and the dashed lines during the 1970s is a measure of the slowdown in the latter decade.

To grasp the full meaning of these charts, a few words of explanation are needed. The scale used to measure the changes in industrial production is a ratio scale designed to facilitate comparisons of rates of change: equal distances stand for equal *percentage* (not absolute) changes, and conversely unequal distances measure unequal percentage changes (e.g., a jump from 100 to 150—50 percent—is half the jump from 50 to 100—100 percent). The advantage of this method appears clearly when we compare the slopes of the dashed lines. Thus, the fact that the 1960–1969

Industrial Production 1960-1980
(1967=100)

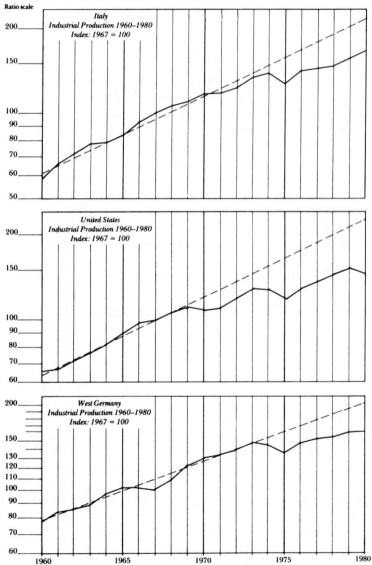

Trend of industrial production during the 1960s — — — — — — —
Annual index of production _____

Ratio scale

Italy
Industrial Production 1960–1980
Index: 1967 = 100

United States
Industrial Production 1960–1980
Index: 1967 = 100

West Germany
Industrial Production 1960–1980
Index: 1967 = 100

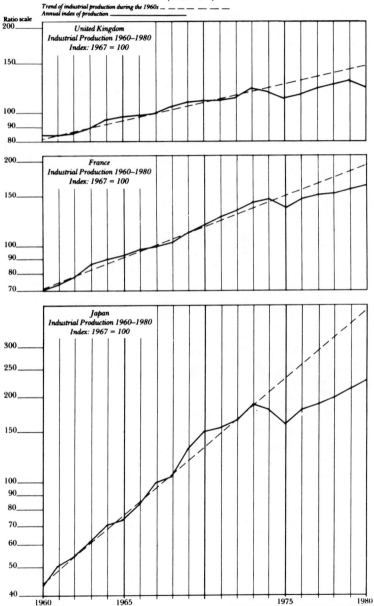

Industrial Production 1960-1980
(1967 = 100)

Trend of industrial production during the 1960s _ _ _ _ _ _
Annual index of production _____

Ratio scale

United Kingdom
Industrial Production 1960–1980
Index: 1967 = 100

France
Industrial Production 1960–1980
Index: 1967 = 100

Japan
Industrial Production 1960–1980
Index: 1967 = 100

1960   1965   1975   1980

trend line for Japan is much steeper than in all the other countries shows that the rate of increase of Japanese production was considerably greater than elsewhere. Similarly, the relatively flat line for the United Kingdom indicates how much its production growth lagged behind the other advanced capitalist nations.

The dissimilarities in national growth rates during the years of prosperity are of course due to a variety of historical and other reasons. They are characteristic of the uneven development among nations (and regions) that permeates the entire history of capitalism. What is relevant to the present purpose are the similarities that prevail despite the differences. What we find in these charts is a fairly steady growth rate in the 1960s followed by a decided retardation in the 1970s. The turning points are not all the same: the United States leads the pack, beginning its departure from the growth trend in 1970, while the others slacken off a few years later. In no case did industrial production sufficiently recover from the 1973–1975 recession to get back to the earlier growth path. Along with the changing growth pattern came two other diseases that spread throughout these countries during the 1970s: the average levels of unemployment shot up, and inflation accelerated.

What all this signifies is the petering out of the forces that had generated the long postwar prosperity wave. In one industry after another there developed a sizable world-wide excess of capacity relative to demand. Although this is most obvious in the case of textiles, steel, shipbuilding, and autos, the signs of overexpansion have been showing up in many other industries as well. Protectionism and cartels are once more on the agenda. Meanwhile, no new forces that could conceivably provide the needed stimuli for a renewed wave of prosperity are visible on the horizon. The combination of persistent idle capacity in the older, established industries and the absence of new industries of sufficient magnitude to pull the economy out of the doldrums explains why capital investment, too, has lagged in the 1970s. The World Bank in its *World Development Report, 1980* calculated that the average annual growth rate of gross domestic investment in the industrialized nations as a whole declined precipitously from 5.6 percent in the 1960s to 1.5 percent from 1970 to 1978 (the latest year for which data were then available). In short, in the past decade and so far in the present one, the world capitalist economy has once again entered a stage of stagnation, with no change in sight.

The question arises as to why this metamorphosis escaped the attention of the establishment economists. Not only did they fail to identify the early warning signals that were visible already in the 1960s, but they have been loath to acknowledge what the coincidence of production retardation, growing unemployment, spiralling inflation, and financial instability really adds up to. Of course, they are not blind. When trouble finally matures in a given area, they recognize it and attempt to account for it.* But generally, the interrelations and interdependence of the critical problems are not explored, beyond looking for a scapegoat (as, for example, the sudden leaps in oil prices) to explain everything.

There are no doubt numerous reasons for the failures of the establishment economists, but the fundamental problem, we believe, is their pro-capitalist bias which results in ignoring the way a capitalist economy operates—the laws of profit-making and of the marketplace, as the fundamental factors causing recurrent crises. Nor for the same reason are they able to distinguish between a cyclical and a general structural crisis.

In addition to the question of bias, it is the very methods used by orthodox economists to analyze and forecast the economy that are at fault. Their econometric models and computer programs—the tools of the trade—are unable to take into account some of the most basic and decisive elements that shape the course of events. These include the inexorable increase in the concentration of economic power, especially its key role in generating the long-run inflationary trend which dates back to the turn of the century; the effect of the U.S. hegemonic position in the imperialistic network and the consequences of the decline of this hegemony; the import of the enormous Eurodollar market; the impact of the multina-

---

*We are discussing the outstanding celebrities of the economics profession as well as the major schools of orthodox thought. There are outstanding exceptions in particular fields, notably the prescient work of Professor Robert Triffin on international money and of Professor Hyman Minsky on domestic finance.

tional corporations and banks; the role of debt in propping up the economy and the resulting fragility of financial institutions and the money market; and, above all, the normal tendency of capitalist economies to stagnation.

In contrast, it is precisely these major themes that provide the focus for the essays collected in this volume.* In addition, a number of the following papers are concerned with the myths and shibboleths promulgated by economists, government leaders, and the business press—false diagnoses that confuse the public and deflect attention from the main causes of economic instability.

One of the persistent illusions of economists is the belief that their advice has been in large measure responsible for guiding the course of the U.S. economy. This is not to deny that government actions have been important, or that the ideas of economists have played a role in shaping them. But an examination of U.S. economic history since the end of the Second World War should disabuse anyone of the notion that the New Economics, about which Professor Samuelson and other leading economists like to boast, has in any way been the decisive factor.

Three major forces underlie the dynamism of the U.S. economy in the twenty-five years following the Second World War: The pent-up internal demand for consumer durables that piled up during the war; U.S hegemony in world capitalism; and the military expenditures incurred and wars waged to support that hegemonic position. While these forces stimulated and sustained growth over a long period, they also, for one reason or another, ultimately petered out as generators of prosperity. When their cumulative effect passed the peak of effectiveness, the tendency to stagnation took over—with or without the economists' bag of tricks.

At the end of the war, the working class, perhaps for the first time in U.S. history, had a sizable accumulation of savings. Sev-

---

*These are also the subject matter of our two earlier books of essays on the course of economic developments: *The Dynamics of U.S. Capitalism: Corporate Structure, Inflation, Credit, Gold, and the Dollar* (Monthly Review Press, 1972), and *The End of Prosperity: The American Economy in the 1970s* (Monthly Review Press, 1977).

eral years of full employment, with extra pay for overtime on war production, had provided a strong flow of consumer income; autos, housing, and other consumer durables had been absent from the market place because of the necessity to free materials and manufacturing capacity for the war machine; and effective price controls had protected the value of the dollar. Moreover, the postwar demand for consumer durables was especially strong not only because of deprivation during the war years but also because of low consumer income during the preceding Great Depression. One need only recall that residential construction fell 80 percent and auto sales 75 percent between 1929 and 1932, both recovering very slowly in the subsequent upturn.

This huge unprecedented reservoir of effective demand was grist for the capitalists' mill. New production facilities were constructed, suburbs developed, roads built—this whole process gathering its own momentum as increased employment and income supported still more growth. The initial impetus, however, soon wore out: it didn't take too many years for the savings of the working class to be used up and for the backlog to be worked off. New props were needed, and these were provided by a rapid expansion of consumer credit, including mortgage money for new housing. Even so, the momentum stemming from a rising demand for consumer durables was bound to weaken sooner or later. The following table (page 18) for the pivotal auto industry, showing the sharply declining rate of growth in demand from 1960 on, illustrates a general pattern.

Of course the postwar prosperity was based on more than the consumer durable goods business. It also fed on the desperate needs of the rest of the world for food, materials, and manufactures. Farms, factories, and homes in war-torn Europe and Asia had been ruined at the same time that the United States had been able greatly to boost its agricultural and industrial capacity. The only limitation on the foreign market for U.S. goods was the lack of gold or dollars in the customers' till. This was soon remedied to an important extent by the means of payment furnished by the Marshall Plan and similar types of aid to allies and client states. Financial obstacles to this generosity had been removed by the Bretton Woods agreement under which the United States had in

Retail Sales of Autos
(Domestic plus Imports)

Period	Average Annual Sales (Millions)	Percent Increase from Previous 5-Year Period
1956–60	5.9	———
1961–65	7.7	30.5%
1966–70	9.1	18.2
1971–75	10.1	11.0
1976–80	10.5	4.0

Source: U.S. Department of Commerce, Business Statistics, 1977 (Washington, D.C.: Superintendent of Documents, 1978) and Survey of Current Business, various issues.

effect been granted a license to print money for use in international trade and finance.

This fitted in well with the design which ideologues of the ruling class visualized as the "American Century." The U.S. predominance in production, trade, and finance, backed by formidable military power straddling the globe, furnished a powerful stimulus to domestic prosperity during the early postwar years. But this too began to wane as other advanced capitalist nations gathered strength, entered into vigorous competition and even overtook the United States in some areas. Thus, while in 1950 U.S. manufacturing output amounted to almost 62 percent of the combined output of the ten leading industrial nations, this share dropped to 50 percent in 1965 and 43 percent by 1976. The U.S. predominance in exports of manufactures also suffered a sharp decline, from about 30 percent of total world exports of manufactures in 1953, to 16 percent in 1965, and only 13 percent in 1976.*

The relative loss of competitive strength in world trade intensified the difficulties connected with the dollar's role as an international currency, thus limiting the ability of the United

*William Branson, Trends in United States International Trade and Investment Since World War II (Cambridge, MA: National Bureau of Economic Research, 1980, "Conference Paper No. 21").

States to take advantage of its hegemonic position by flooding world markets with dollars. Although the international role of the dollar is still important in propping up the domestic economy, new elements of restraint emerged as a result of the severe beating the dollar took in foreign-exchange markets during the 1970s. The upshot is that although the United States is still more or less the leading power in the imperialist system, its decline from clear-cut hegemony has meant the weakening of this factor as a stimulus to economic growth.

The third major stimulant to the economy came from the growth of military expenditures. There were two major leaps, the first associated with the Korean War and the second with the Vietnamese war. At the time of the Korean War, a decision was made to develop a major war-production sector as a permanent feature of the economy. As a result of this program, which was additional to supplying arms for Korean operations, military spending rose from less than 5 percent of the 1950 Gross National Product to over 13 percent in 1953. By the time the Vietnamese war came around, a huge military production program was already in operation. As a result, the increased demand needed to supply the forces in Vietnam did not show up as a significant increase in the ratio of arms expenditures to GNP. But its economic impact was nevertheless important, as can be seen from the fact that during the latter half of the 1960s military expenditures were equal to 89 percent of business spending on plant and equipment.

Both of these step-ups were thus strategic to economic growth during the years in which they occurred. But supplying a military establishment, no matter how large, cannot by itself provide the stimulation needed to prevent economic growth rates from declining. As in the case of the two expansionary forces discussed above, this one too did not prevent the economy's drift into stagnation in the 1970s.

It is of course important to understand that stagnation did not suddenly make an appearance in the 1970s. Actually, the tendency to stagnation has existed throughout the postwar period. From time to time, expansionary forces helped overcome this tendency, and when these forces were mutually supportive, growth accelerated. But at times some of the contributors to rapid growth slowed up, even before they reached the peak of their influence. It was on such occasions that a fresh injection of credit either helped tide things over or gave a new fillip to growth. As early as the 1950s, the conditions under which instalment credit was provided for the purchase of autos were loosened. From 1954 to 1957 banks and finance companies reduced down payments and extended repayment periods for such loans from two to three years. Later in the 1970s repayment schedules were stretched even further—to four and five years. It was also in the 1950s that mortgage terms were eased; in some parts of the country even down payments were eliminated. Each of these changes naturally invigorated sales by drawing in customers who otherwise could not afford to buy cars and houses.

The growth of debt as an increasingly important prop to business met with many obstacles. In particular, government and Federal Reserve regulations stood in the way. Reacting to the general financial collapse and numerous bank failures during the Great Depression, federal authorities had instituted a variety of regulations and controls designed to assure future financial stability. Later on, in the changed climate of the postwar years, these restraints came to be seen as roadblocks preventing banks and other lenders from meeting the growing demand of business and consumers for a freer flow of credit. The restraints were gradually relaxed but not rapidly enough to satisfy the financial community. Under these circumstances, and as profit-making opportunities arising from the needs of borrowers burgeoned, banks and other types of financial institutions became increasingly ingenious in creating new institutions and money market instruments designed to thwart or circumvent government restraints.

It was this combination of greater business reliance on debt and increasingly aggressive lending practices that eventually led to a series of crises or near-crises in financial markets. These, called "credit crunches" in the trade, have been showing up with increasing frequency. The first occurred in 1966, followed by more severe periods of strain in 1969–70, 1974, and 1979–80.*

---

*A useful and illuminating review of these developments can be found in an article by an official of the First Boston Corporation: Albert M. Wojnilower, "The

The growing severity of financial instability resulted not only from periodic drying up of the supply of credit (relative to demand), but from bankruptcies or the threat of bankruptcies in situations where potential chain reactions could bring about disaster in the financial community as a whole: Penn Central in 1970; Franklin National Bank and many real estate investment trusts in 1974; the Hunt brothers, First Pennsylvania Bank, and Chrysler in 1980.

Disaster was avoided each time mainly by emergency injections of money, either directly by the Federal Reserve to banks, or by government subsidies, loans, or loan guarantees for ailing firms or industries. These actions, in turn, broadened the base for a renewed expansion of debt, more inflation, and greater dependency of the economy as a whole on a ballooning of credit.

As on many previous occasions in the history of capitalism, the aggressive operations of financial institutions in the midst of skyrocketing inflation spurred a new era of speculation. And this too, perhaps this especially, has magnified the financial turbulence of recent years. Greenspan pinpoints the new threat in the area of housing:

> The excesses [in speculation] lie elsewhere [than in the stock market], particularly in the housing market. It's there, if anywhere, that speculative imbalances have surfaced which could threaten the stability of the American economy. Financed by elephantine advances in mortgage debt, residential real estate values have soared. The market value of the average home has nearly tripled in little more than a decade. . . . The cumulative impact [of potential problems arising from such speculation] would be far deeper than any envisioned recession.*

Central Role of Credit Crunches in Recent Financial History," in *Brookings Papers on Economic Activity*, No. 2, 1980. See also, "Banks: Skating on Thin Ice," in Harry Magdoff and Paul Sweezy, *The End of Prosperity: The American Economy in the 1970s* (New York: Monthly Review Press, 1977).

*"The Great Malaise," *Challenge*, March/April 1980. In addition to the dangers inherent in the speculative housing market, Greenspan discusses in this article the possibility of a collapse in the world financial market that could be brought about by defaults on loans to the Third World and by stresses associated with the huge Eurodollar float.

A speculative mania has gripped other sectors as well. For example, the number of contracts traded on commodity-futures exchanges in 1980 was more than four and one-half times that of 1970. The gambling spirit has spurred the invention and spread of new types of speculative trading in which well-heeled corporations and individuals participate: stock options, foreign currencies, interest rate futures. Almost all of these newer forms of gambling got their start or came into full bloom in the 1970s, just when the stagnation tendencies in production took over. By now, the volume of speculative trading in futures of all kinds (commodities, precious metals, financial instruments, and currencies) exceeds $2 trillion a year.

What does it all add up to? The path of U.S. economic development sketched in this introduction and elaborated on in the essays that follow has led to a constant narrowing of options. The measures adopted to cope with stagnation and avoid a major depression have increased inflation, dependence on debt, speculation, and financial instability. But along this road there is no escape, only closer and closer approach to the precipice.

Faced with this menacing situation, the powers that be tend to grasp at straws, seeking miracle cures, fleeing forward into foreign adventures, and looking to safeguard their profits by taking it out of the hide of the working class, the poor, and the old. The latest moves in this direction are the subject of the two concluding essays in this volume.

1.
Steel and Stagnation

The upward swing of the business cycle is rarely smooth. Some industries and regions generally expand more rapidly than others, and all sorts of disproportionalities typically emerge. There is, however, something strikingly different in the unevenness of the current recovery. For this time it is the crucial steel industry—the supplier of raw materials for the construction, capital goods, and consumer durables industries—that is not merely lagging behind but in serious trouble. So much so that the staid *New York Times,* surely no scaremonger when it comes to reporting business news, headlined a recent major article, "Crisis Deepening in American Steel." (September 29, 1977)

The cry of crisis may be an exaggeration at this stage, but there need be little wonder that the business community and Washington are alarmed over recent developments. The general recovery from the recession low in the first quarter of 1975 has been advancing in fits and starts, and each little setback in the index of industrial production or other economic indicators stimulates fears that a new recession may be at hand. Still, hope remains that each upturn will soon find a surer footing, especially in the private investment sector. After all, weren't all previous post-Second World War recoveries spurred on and sustained by an upsurge of capital investment, including the key ingredient of an expansion of steel production capacity?

But this time one steel company after another, instead of adding to capacity, has begun to *reduce* it—right in the middle of the prosperity phase of the cycle. Bethlehem Steel Corporation and

This article originally appeared in the November 1977 issue of *Monthly Review.*

Armco Steel Corporation, both among the industry's top five producers, have closed down steel operations in Johnstown, Pa., Lackawanna, N.Y., and Middletown, Ohio. Youngstown Sheet and Tube has reduced steel-making operations in its home base of Youngstown, Ohio, by 75 percent. Other capacity cutbacks have been announced by Kaiser Steel Corporation and U.S. Steel. Industry spokesmen and Wall Street specialists believe that more plant shutdowns are in the offing, a not surprising conclusion in view of the fact that in mid-September the working steel mills were operating at about 75 percent of capacity. This has meant that in addition to the firings resulting from the closing down of plants, a large number of blue- and white-collar workers have been laid off in those still remaining in operation.

Steel company executives unanimously put the blame for these developments on the recent acceleration in the rate of steel imports. But this self-serving argument, while not devoid of a factual basis, only beclouds the real issues. For although it is mainly in the last few months that the steel industry's troubles have reached proportions critical enough to induce drastic actions, the underlying forces leading to the present situation have been building up for some time. Moreover, the roots of the problem go much deeper than the allegedly "unfair" competition from Japanese and European imports that the U.S. industry complains about. In fact, the rising tide of steel imports is itself a reflection of a more basic and long-maturing crisis of the steel industry throughout the capitalist world.

What needs to be emphasized here is that each of the leading capitalist nations is striving to cope with a common problem: excess steel capacity in the face of stagnant *world* demand. And one way of coping is to try to take over markets in other countries. Steel plants, it should be noted, are idle not only in the United States but in England, Germany, France and Japan as well. As far as Western Europe is concerned, the *New York Times* reported earlier this year (May 23): "From Lancashire in Britain through Belgium and the French Lorraine to the German industrial heartland of the Ruhr, Europe's steel-makers are now experiencing their worst crisis in living memory." This "round-up" dispatch then goes on to explain:

Even if the world economy revives, prospects for the European steel industry may not improve very much. There are signs that world demand for steel is no longer growing as fast as it used to.

By 1970, per capita steel consumption in the industrial countries had climbed to 1,400 pounds a year from only 200 pounds in 1910. But since then it has leveled off, even when economic times were good.

"We now have too many ships, enough roads and bridges, and masses of office buildings," warns Sir Charles Villiers [Chairman of the British Steel Corporation].

Japan alone now has idle plants capable of turning out 30 million tons of steel a year, or nearly a quarter of annual Common Market production. In Europe, the O.E.C.D. calculates, steel demand would need to grow by 10 percent for five years to get the steel industry working at 80 percent capacity.

The background to the current steel situation is highlighted in Table 1-1. Significantly, the general up-and-down contours are similar in each of the advanced capitalist areas; differences are in the rates of change. The seven years before the peak of the world capitalist boom (1973) were on the whole a period of rapidly expanding output; and to make these increases possible, new steel-producing capacity had to be installed. While data on capacity are not readily available for all the countries, the well-informed *Business Week* (September 19) estimates that the combined capacity of these three areas was about 440 million metric tons in 1973, or some 40 million tons of crude steel more than they produced in that year.* This 10 percent margin of excess capacity at the peak of the boom is in large part accounted for by the fact that steel-making capacity was being rapidly created in anticipation of a continuation of past rates of economic growth throughout the world capitalist system, with full awareness that such capacity would for a while be in excess of current demand.

As can be seen from Table 1-1, however, the recession reversed the strong upward movement in all three areas. During 1975 as a

---

*The data on capacity are calculated from a chart in the *Business Week* article, which compares capacity and consumption. The chart presents the data in short tons, which we have converted to metric tons for comparability with the statistics in Table 1-1.

Table 1-1
Steel Production
(Ingots of Crude Steel in Millions of Metric Tons)

	United States	European Economic Community[a]	Japan
1966	121.7	108.5	47.0
1969	128.2	132.6	80.9
1973	136.8	147.5	117.8
1975	105.8	123.6	101.3
1976	116.3	133.8	107.4
1977[b]	112.1	128.4	110.2

(a)   Includes Belgium, Denmark, France, German Federal Republic, Ireland, Luxemburg, Netherlands, and United Kingdom.

(b)   Average of first five months at an annual rate. The production data for 1976 were multiplied by the percentage change between the first six months of 1976 and the first six months of 1977, in order to eliminate the effect of seasonal variation.

Source: United Nations, *Yearbook of Industrial Statistics,* 1975 edition, vol. 2, and United Nations, *Monthly Bulletin of Statistics,* August 1977.

whole, a year in which recovery from the recession was already under way, the combined production for the three areas was still about 18 percent below the peak. The decline in 1974 and early 1975, although doubtless more severe than anticipated, could hardly have come as a surprise to the capitalists in such a quintessentially cyclical industry as steel. But what was surely unexpected was the uncharacteristic sluggishness of the recovery. During the first five months of 1977 production in each one of the areas was still below the 1973 peak. Thus, *in the third year of recovery* the combined steel production of the leading capitalist centers was still approximately 13 percent below the peak.*

---

*The cyclical pattern of the 1970s has generally been typical of the rest of the capitalist world (mainly European countries outside the Common Market, plus Canada and Australia). The exceptions (notably India, Brazil, South Africa, South Korea, and Mexico) were countries engaged in the main in building up a relatively small, native steel-making capability with which to replace imports. The experience of the centrally planned economies, on the other hand, was strikingly

This, however, is only part of the story: steel capacity as distinct from production kept on growing throughout both the recession and the exceptionally weak recovery. According to the *Business Week* estimates referred to above, the crude capacity of the steel mills in the United States, Western Europe, and Japan advanced from 440 million metric tons in 1973 to over 500 million tons in 1976. An increase of capacity in the midst of stagnation is not unprecedented and was probably due to one or more of the following reasons: (1) capacity additions started before the recession were completed in subsequent years; (2) some steel-mill expansions may have been started after 1973 in the expectation that a new boom would soon follow; and (3) technical improvements increased the production capability of pre-existing equipment. Whatever the reason, the fact remains that steel producers in the three areas shown in Table 1-1 were operating in the opening months of this year with some 30 percent of their capacity idle. And the consequence has been—as it necessarily must be in any industry like steel in which overhead costs are especially large—a severe cut in profit rates running to actual losses by some of the weaker companies.

This critical juncture in the affairs of the capitalist world's steel industry results essentially from a contradiction between the incessant drive of the steel producers to accumulate more capital (as a source of still more profits) on the one hand and the onset of stagnation in the economy as a whole on the other.

The expansionist drive has been especially in evidence in the Japanese and European Common Market industries that have been geared since the early 1950s to above-normal growth rates, which in turn have depended in considerable measure on constantly finding and building for new export markets. And here we meet what is now revealing itself as one of the most paradoxical features of the international economic order established under

---

different from the dominant tendencies in the capitalist countries. For several years before the latest recession, steel production in the USSR and the United States had been running neck-and-neck. Since the 1973 peak in the United States, however, the USSR has been increasing production each year, thus outdistancing the United States and becoming the largest steel producer in the world.

U.S. hegemony at the end of the Second World War. A very important ingredient of this set-up was the wide-spread dismantling of the system of tariffs and other restrictions on international trade which had characterized the 1930s. American capitalists assumed that the main beneficiaries of this process of trade liberalization would be U.S. export industries, and for a considerable period this was indeed the case. In addition, trade liberalization was an essential part of a more comprehensive set of international relations which favored U.S. foreign investment and the supremacy of U.S. finance (including the enthronement of the dollar as the reserve currency of the capitalist world). The other side of this coin of course was the opening up of U.S. markets (and those of other advanced capitalist countries) to a freer flow of imports.

As long as the capitalist world economy continued to grow, this arrangement worked to the advantage of all the advanced industrial countries. They interpenetrated each other's territory both through exports and through direct investment, but as long as markets were generally expanding from one year to the next the big multinational monopolies gained far more than they lost. This situation began to change as soon as overall expansion gave way to stagnation, and this change was nowhere more marked than in the steel industry. As already noted, the European and

Table 1-2
Consumption of Steel Mill Products by U.S. Manufacturers

	Millions of Short Tons
1965	67.0
1970	67.5
1973	81.2
1974	79.0
1975	62.1
1976	62.9
1977 (1st half, annual rate)	65.8

Source: Data prior to 1975: U.S. Department of Commerce, *Business Statistics* (The Biennial Supplement of the *Survey of Current Business*), 1975. Data for 1975 and after: *Survey of Current Business*, July 1977.

Japanese steel industries were heavily dependent on exports all along. When adversity struck simultaneously throughout the world capitalist economy, therefore, it was only natural that they should cast a hungrier eye than usual on the huge U.S. market.

When the U.S. demand for steel was expanding, as in the preceding years, an invasion of American markets by Japanese and European steel producers was annoying to the U.S. industry but hardly the disaster it is now perceived to be. The reality today, however, is very different. With the whole U.S. economy stagnating, the demand for steel in the United States sharply *contracted.* Dramatic evidence of this can be seen in Table 1-2 which shows the consumption of steel-mill products by U.S. manufacturing industries in the period of 1965–1977 (manufacturing normally accounts for about 60 percent of total steel usage, the remainder going mainly to construction, mining, and railroads). What is most startling about the data shown in Table 1-2 is the absence of any significant recovery at all in 1976 and early 1977, *with 1976–1977 levels still below those of 1965.* Lacking a detailed study of the recent behavior of the demand for steel, we can only guess that the main reason for the divergence between it and the general increase in manufacturing activity in the current phase of the cycle lies first in the trend toward smaller and lighter automobiles, and second in the increasing substitution of other materials such as aluminum and plastics for many items formerly made with steel.

Be that as it may, the implications of the sagging demand for steel are clear enough. Recovery for this key industry would require a much more rapidly expanding economy than has thus

Table 1-3
Expenditures for Fixed Investment

	Billions of Constant (1972) Dollars
First Quarter 1973 (previous peak)	193.2
Second Quarter, 1975 (trough)	148.9
Second Quarter, 1977	184.0

Source: Survey of Current Business, various issues.

far taken place or seems to be on the horizon. The September 19th issue of *Business Week* put the matter succinctly: "Anything short of a record-breaking capital boom would still leave the steel industry in the doldrums." And this, of course, is where the dog is buried. The story on capital investment is briefly summarized in Table 1-3. The most recent high point for investment in residential and non-residential structures and equipment occurred in the first quarter of 1973, when $193.2 billion (in 1972 dollars) was laid out for such purposes. This figure declined by 23 percent to the low reached in the second quarter of 1975. After two years of recovery, capital investment is still 5 percent below the previous peak. This performance is hardly the precursor of the kind of "record-breaking capital boom" which *Business Week* sees as the necessary condition for overcoming a sluggish steel market.

With the U.S. steel industry thus in deep trouble, with stagnation prevailing in the rest of the capitalist world, and with some of the Third World countries trying to build up steel industries of their own, the major steel producers here and abroad have been turning more and more to the age-old solutions big business adopts or promotes in times of crisis. The first is the rationalization of domestic industry through mergers and a reduction in capacity, thus creating the conditions for artificial shortages and higher prices. The second is to establish cartels dividing up internal and external markets. And the third is to gain protection from foreign competition by building higher tariff walls and devising other barriers to imports. These devices of monopoly capital have one purpose in common: to provide a framework for achieving higher profits by reducing competition and facilitating control over prices and production. But by the same token, they contribute to further stagnation—and, by generating more unemployment and higher prices, worsen the living conditions of the people.

We should, of course, recognize that the steel industry has some special problems and is not—at least not yet—representative of what is happening in the rest of the economy. On the other hand, because of its intricate ties with other decisive sectors, it is in an especially influential position. We will hardly go wrong if we see in current developments in steel a harbinger of events to come with the continuing deepening of stagnation in this era of monopoly capital.

2.
Multinational Corporations and Banks

Multinational Corporations (MNCs) are forms and mechanisms of imperialism, not its essence. This of course does not mean that they are unimportant. Imperialism could not exist without appropriate forms and mechanisms. In what follows we shall be discussing imperialism in the period since the Second World War, and MNCs are both products and necessary conditions of the way it has developed and its mode of operation in this stage.

This should not be taken to imply, however, that MNCs are inventions or innovations of this stage. They have historic roots going back to the earliest days of the global capitalist system (and it must never be forgotten that capitalism has *always* been a global system, never one confined to individual states or territories).

Are MNCs really "multinational"? The answer is yes and no. They are in the sense that they operate in more than one, and often many, nations. Exxon (formerly Standard Oil of New Jersey), for example, has around 300 subsidiaries in more than 50 countries. But as far as their ownership and control are concerned, MNCs are strictly national—U.S., British, Dutch, Swiss, French, German, Japanese. The largest number are U.S.-owned and controlled, but on a per capita basis the United Kingdom and probably also the Netherlands and Switzerland are still ahead of the United States. (There are two MNCs which are bi-national in respect to ownership and control, Royal Dutch/Shell and Uni-

This is an abbreviated version of a paper delivered at an international symposium on imperialism at the University of Barcelona, May 9–11, 1977. It originally appeared in the January 1978 issue of *Monthly Review*.

lever, which have complicated managerial structures centered in both Britain and Holland. But these are among the oldest of MNCs, and their example has never been copied in recent years.)

In what my colleague Harry Magdoff has aptly called the Age of Imperialism (roughly the last hundred years), the pioneer MNCs were the oil companies, especially Standard Oil and Royal Dutch/Shell. From the outset in the case of Shell and increasingly in that of Standard (largely, to be sure, because of the competitive struggle with Shell) multinationality was forced on them by geological conditions, that is to say, by the location of accessible and recoverable underground petroleum reserves. In more recent times, and especially since the Second World War, geography has been less important and the imperatives of monopolistic business strategy more important. A corporation starts with an export market and then, to protect it from competition, moves to assemble and then manufacture its products on the spot—*if it doesn't, someone else will.* Added reasons, according to circumstances, are to take advantage of cheap labor supplies and to get behind tariff barriers and other types of import restrictions. It is worth noting that the transition from colonialism to neocolonialism, which has taken place almost entirely in the post-Second World War period, greatly strengthened these reasons for going multinational. British firms needed less protection against foreign competitors in the old Empire, and neocolonies are likely to place more restrictions on imports than old-fashioned colonies were permitted to do.

It also needs to be emphasized that it is really only very large corporations of the kind that have developed in recent decades that have the financial and managerial resources to move freely on the international scene: smaller corporations might like to but find it beyond their means. So for all these reasons MNCs could only come into their own at a fairly advanced stage of monopoly capitalism. It is therefore not surprising that the very term "multinational corporation" is a product of the post-Second World War period. I have not been able to find it in the literature before 1960, and I think its common usage can plausibly be said to date from the publication in 1963 by the U.S. magazine *Business Week* of a special supplement entitled "Multinational Corporations."

So far as imperialism is concerned, our main interest in MNCs naturally focuses on their role in the Third World. Nevertheless, one can understand them better if one first takes note of some of their characteristic activities within the advanced imperialist countries. Here there is a strong and persistent tendency toward *interpenetration* of each other's territory. This fact has been obscured by the special conditions which existed in the years immediately after the Second World War. At that time U.S. corporations were the only ones in a position to move freely on the international stage: the other advanced capitalist countries were much too preoccupied with the difficult problems of recovery and reconstruction. As more and more U.S. corporations moved into Europe, especially after the establishment of the Common Market, it began to appear that the MNC was a specifically American instrument for establishing hegemony over the imperialist center as well as over the dependent colonies and neocolonies of the periphery. More recently, however, we can see that this is not really so. European and Japanese corporations have the same reasons for wanting to establish branches and subsidiaries in the United States as U.S. corporations have for invading Europe and Japan. And indeed MNCs from all the advanced capitalist countries have been moving into each other's territory in recent years, and this is especially marked in the case of movement *into* the United States since the beginning of the world recession in 1973. The U.S. business and financial press has been carrying more and more reports of such movement by European and Japanese corporations in the last few years. The reason is basically simple: the more markets an oligopolist is represented in, the stronger will be its competitive position vis-à-vis rivals in each and every one of them.

We turn now to MNCs and the Third World. That they have implanted themselves all over the Third World is obvious, and that as a result all sorts of processing and manufacturing activities are now carried on in the Third World that were absent before the era of the MNC is also obvious. Many observers have interpreted this as marking a transformation in the nature of imperialism and the beginning of a process of independent economic development in the Third World. And this theory has been

advanced not only by bourgeois social scientiests and apologists
for imperialism but also by some Marxists (see, for example,
the well-known article "Imperialism and Capitalist Industrialization," by Bill Warren, a British Marxist, in *New Left Review,*
October 1973).

The important question here is not whether MNCs have brought
modern industry to the Third World—that is undeniable—but
whether in doing so they have initiated a process of *independent*
development. And the answer, I think, is definitely no. MNCs
establish factories in the Third World to produce for markets
which already exist, not for markets which they expect their
activities to create. And what are these already existing markets?
Basically they are of two kinds: (1) the consumption requirements
of the small, local, upper-income groups (local bourgeoisie, landowners, state functionaries, military officers, etc.) which have
traditionally imported their luxury goods; and (2) international
markets in which demand comes from outside the countries in
question.* Demand coming from workers, peasants, unemployed,
etc.—i.e., the vast majority of the population—plays a minor part
in this process. The MNCs, in other words, produce for a domestic
market limited to a small proportion of the population, plus an
international market dependent on developments outside the
country. The great mass of the people figure in this picture solely
as a cost factor which it is in the interest of the MNCs as well as in
that of the local upper-income groups to keep as cheap as possible.
Capitalist industrialization in the Third World therefore goes
hand in hand with ruthless exploitation of the country's human
resources, which in many cases actually drives real wages below
the subsistence-determined value of labor power and threatens
the very reproduction of the labor force. The appropriate, indeed necessary, political complement to this type of economic
development is the brutal military-police dictatorship which is

---

*In some cases (e.g., Brazil) the demand created by expenditures of the state,
which of course is controlled by the local upper-income groups and their foreign
allies, also becomes important; and this will perhaps be increasingly the case in the
future. But this added element does not change the nature of the basic argument.

fast becoming the norm throughout the capitalist-dominated regions of Asia, Africa, and Latin America.*

The pattern of economic development we have been discussing is in sharp contrast with the one which characterizes the advanced capitalist countries where mass markets based on rising real wages and a large capital-goods sector have always been the leading factors. In the Third World, instead, the leading role is taken by luxury goods and exports, which means that these countries are incapable of initiating or shaping an independent course of development. Their dependence includes the copying or borrowing of consumption styles, hence *cultural* dependence, and of course (via the MNCs) *technological* dependence. One of the most characteristic features of this pattern of dependent development is the hothouse growth of tourism, which becomes a favored province of MNCs such as airlines and hotel companies, and often is an important earner of foreign exchange, acting in this way similarly to export industries. Tourism also acts as a carrier of cultural styles and values and as a corrupter of significant strata of the populations in the host countries.

Third World countries experiencing the kind of dependent development we have been discussing may display very rapid rates of increase of Gross National Product, at the very same time that the material condition of the mass of the people remains stagnant or even declines. The growth industries in the area of luxury goods and exports may *look* very big and modern, but they are highly capital-intensive, pollute the environment, and pro-

---

*In a fuller treatment of this subject, the analysis would have to be qualified to take account of the capital goods required by the Third World industrialization process. Production of luxury and export goods involves relatively sophisticated technology which at the outset is imported in the form not only of blueprints but also of actual means of production. Later on, however, the MNCs may elect to produce these means of production locally, which means establishing a capital-goods industry. The fact that the latter does not have a mass consumption-goods industry to produce for—a dominant feature of the development process in the metropolitan countries—means that the capital-goods industry (Department I of Marx's reproduction scheme) must remain stunted and incapable of employing more than a very limited number of workers.

vide relatively few jobs for workers and no benefits at all for peasants and the marginalized unemployed. Brazil is perhaps the outstanding "success" story of this kind of MNC-led economic development. GNP growth rates in the period since the military coup of 1964 have often attained 10 percent or more, among the highest in the world.* But in the same period real wages have actually declined by as much as 30 to 40 percent. The president of Brazil, on a visit to Washington a few years ago, summed up the situation in a brilliant aphorism when he said that in his country the economy was doing fine but the people weren't.

Further important aspects of dependent development under the auspices of MNCs are that a significant part of the local bourgeoisie is in effect denationalized and co-opted into the service of foreign interests, while much of the surplus product of the national economies is drained away in the form of repatriated profits, service of foreign debts, royalty payments for foreign technology, false invoicing of imports and exports, and the building up of Swiss bank accounts by the local rich, fearful for the future of their own countries.

One might ask whether, in the final analysis, there is *anything* positive about this kind of MNC-led economic development. And my answer would be, yes, there are at least two positive aspects. *First,* among the massive cultural imports by the Third World from the advanced capitalist countries has been the new world-view which is undeniably the product of the experience of the European proletariat in the eighteenth and nineteenth centuries. This world-view is called Marxism. Its revolutionary essence has often been forgotten or distorted, especially in its lands of origin. But transplanted to the periphery of the global capitalist system where exploitation and suffering have been most severe and the benefits of development smallest, Marxism has had a rebirth. And it is precisely in conditions of maximum MNC power and influence that Marxism has experienced its most significant advances. We now know that the only possible salvation for the great

---

*This of course changed with the onset of the world recession in 1973, but that is a story which does not concern us here.

majority of humanity which lives in the Third World is *not* through reforms of the capitalist system but through a revolutionary rupture of the relations of dependence we have been discussing. Only through such a revolutionary break can a new pattern of development centered on the welfare of the real producing classes be initiated. This is an idea whose time has come, and an idea whose time has come can be an enormously powerful force. And *second,* while the development of industry under MNC dominance has benefited few and injured many, it nevertheless has brought to many lands knowledge and experience of the elements of modern technology and has produced a working class which, even if small, has a crucially important leadership potential, first as a revolutionary force to overthrow the old order, and second as a constructive force to build the new.

Let me now turn, all too briefly, to the subject of Multinational Banks (MNBs). Here, too, we have to do with what is not a new phenomenon. In the period of British imperialist hegemony, London-based banks spread throughout the Empire and in many parts of the dependent world like Latin America, mostly as hand-maidens of British business interests and British colonial administrations and personnel. But in the period since the Second World War, MNBs have taken on a new dimension and a new role. This development has coincided with the explosive proliferation of what have come to be known as Eurodollars and petrodollars.

Allow me to try to explain these terms as simply as possible. By the end of the Second World War the USSR had acquired a considerable sum of dollars which the Soviet leaders did not want to deposit in the United States for fear that the U.S. government, on one pretext or another, would confiscate them. So the dollars were deposited in banks in the city of London, the center of European finance. Thus was born the phenomenon of offshore dollar deposits.

The baby grew to be a giant in the years after the Second World War as the U.S. balance of payments ran persistent deficits, i.e., more dollars went out of the United States than came in. Since the dollar was widely used as a reserve currency in those days—in the popular saying, it was "as good as gold"—a large part of this outflow was added to offshore dollar deposits, and big U.S. banks set up branches in London and elsewhere to accept them, and of course to lend them out at interest to foreign and sometimes domestic U.S. borrowers. Later, after the great increase in the price of oil in 1973, a new flood of dollars from the United States and other countries to pay for petroleum imports flowed into the major oil-exporting countries, especially those of the Middle East. A large part of these, now dubbed petrodollars, was added to the volume of offshore dollar deposits, and the number of banks participating in the business jumped by leaps and bounds.

To these developments must be added another which is not so easy to explain. Within a country, the banking system through its lending activity creates deposit money amounting to some multiple of the reserves which it is constrained, either by law or by custom, to maintain against possible withdrawals. If its reserves increase, it creates more money by a factor of, say, ten (assuming reserve requirements are 10 percent of deposits). The point here is that the same process of creating deposit money operates in an international banking system such as that which has grown up around the Eurodollar. There is, however, this difference, that the lack of any overall regulatory authority and the secrecy (and ignorance) which prevail in the Eurodollar market make it impossible to achieve any precise knowledge about either the total of Eurodollars in existence or the proportion which may have been created by the banks themselves. The aggregate amount of offshore deposits has been *estimated* at over $300 billion, and it is probably safe enough to assume that the amount created by the banks themselves runs into the tens of billions.

What are the consequences and implications of this unprecedented explosion of multinational banking, most of which has taken place in the last ten years? Here I can do no more than list a few of the most important.

First, as far as the big U.S. banks are concerned it has meant an enormous increase in their profits from overseas businesses, hence also a growing vulnerability to global economic conditions and disturbances in the international monetary mechanism. In some cases, notably that of Citibank, the second largest U.S. bank, up to 80 percent of profits come from foreign lending, mostly through their affiliates in London, Singapore, Panama, the Bahamas, the Cayman Islands, and other places where they can establish branches and affiliates free of regulation, and subject only to minimal taxation.

Second, multinational banking is certainly a factor in generating inflation on a global scale, though there is no agreement among the experts on just how important this is.

Third, from the outset, but most markedly since the oil crisis of 1973, the MNBs have loaned large amounts of money to countries with balance-of-payments problems—and, apart from the oil-exporting countries, there are few which have not had such problems. It has now reached the point where many of these debtor countries (including even a developed one like Italy) are at or near the limits of their borrowing capacity. This situation holds the potential of two types of crisis: (a) of the borrowing countries which may be thrown into default and faced with catastrophic internal crises because of inability to import supplies on which they have become heavily dependent; and (b) of the multinational banks themselves, threatened in their turn by defaults of borrowers which, possibly in conjunction with other factors, could trigger a general collapse of the international credit and payments system comparable to that which overwhelmed the capitalist world in 1929-1931.

The situation is grave, if not yet desperate. It is superimposed on the global recession and the deteriorating condition of the Third World discussed earlier, and it underlines for all with eyes to see the urgency not of palliatives and reforms which touch only the surface, but of a revolutionary break with a world order which has outlived its day and threatens the world with more and worse catastrophes in the years ahead.

3.
Emerging Currency and
Trade Wars

Newspaper reports on fluctuations of the U.S. dollar on foreign currency exchanges have been moving up from their customary place in the back business section to front-page prominence. This increasing newsworthiness reflects a growing awareness that the almost year-long downward slide in the international value of the dollar is not simply a technical adjustment or a temporary by-product of money market speculation. In reality the gyrations of the international currency markets are surface manifestations of a growing trade rivalry among the leading capitalist nations, the result of a competitive struggle that has been warming up ever since the long post-Second World War prosperity wave of world capitalism began to subside. The manipulation of exchange rates in the ensuing stage of stagnation has been both cause and effect of a spreading protectionism which shows all the classic signs of impending trade wars.

Before discussing the more basic aspects of these developments it will be useful to review a few elementary facts about the recent movements of the U.S. dollar in international markets. First of all we need to be aware that the dollar has been declining only in relation to a small number of other currencies. If we examine the exchange rates of currencies reported every day in the *Wall Street Journal,* we find that in 1977 as a whole the value of the dollar remained roughly the same or even rose with respect to thirty-three of the forty-three countries listed. The reason is that some of these countries peg their currencies to the U.S. dollar, while

This article originally appeared in the February 1978 issue of *Monthly Review.*

others have devalued their currencies as much as or more than the dollar depreciated last year. Between the first weeks of January 1977 and January 1978, the value of the dollar declined relative to *only ten* of the countries listed—and these were notably the major competitors of the United States in world trade (Japan and the countries of Western Europe, plus some others which are more or less in the currency blocs of these rival trading nations).

What has been happening to the U.S. dollar during 1977 has thus been the result of currency maneuvers (involving, of course, speculation and the "normal" workings of foreign exchange markets) that concern primarily economic relations among the leading capitalist nations, and in particular among the three most powerful—the United States, Germany, and Japan.

The sinking dollar (relative to the currencies of its major trade rivals) has the obvious advantage of strengthening U.S. export opportunities in the affected countries, and at the same time weakening the competitive status of the latter's exports to the United States. Two hypothetical examples will help explain how it works. Take the case of a Japanese manufacturer who a year ago sold his product in the United States for $100. Because of the decline in the dollar relative to the Japanese yen, this manufacturer would now have to sell the item for $124 to earn the same amount of yen as he did a year ago. Conversely, consider the case of an American manufacturer who exports to Germany. If he sold a product there a year ago for 236 marks he would have received $100 in U.S. currency. Today he could cut the price of his product to 206 marks and still take in $100.

One should not, however, overestimate the influence of exchange rates on a country's foreign trade opportunities during periods of vigorously expanding world trade, such as characterized the 1950s and most of the 1960s. As long as the domestic economics of the trading nations were growing fairly rapidly, the expansion of each one's internal markets, taken together with the flexibility in production afforded by advanced industrialization and a well developed technological research capability, could make up for aberrations or imbalances in exchange rates; during such periods of growth, competitive disadvantages in export opportunities for one group of products could be compensated by advantages in others. But as the capitalist world economy moved into a stage of stagnation, and foreign trade openings began to shrink or even disappear, the rivalry for markets took on a new aspect. Each one of the capitalist nations sought, and continues to seek, the way out of its troubles by increasing exports. But they can't all do it successfully at the same time, and most assuredly not during world-wide recessions or periods of sluggish recovery. It is then that the relative exchange rates of national currencies become increasingly important weapons of competition for export markets.

At the same time it is clear that the reduction in the value of a country's currency will not stimulate exports if the currencies of competitors decline in the same proportion. The trick is to devalue one's currency while the exchange rates of one's trading partners' currencies stay the same or, better still, go up. And it is precisely this strategy that has dominated U.S. maneuvering in international currency affairs ever since the end of the 1960s, especially with respect to the value of the dollar compared with that of the German mark or the Japanese yen. The strategy worked in the early 1970s (the dollar was twice devalued simultaneously with an increase in the mark and the yen relative to the dollar) because the United States, as the head of the world imperialist financial and military network, was able to impose its will on its partners-cum-rivals.

It wasn't an easy victory, however, since the United States was at the same time forced to give up some of its hegemonic rights and powers. Nor did the solution of the international financial crisis of the early 1970s alleviate the stresses of inter-imperialist rivalries for very long. The imbalances began to reveal themselves in even more drastic form during the past two years, most notably in the enormous increase in the 1977 deficit in the U.S. balance of payments. This can be seen from an examination of the data presented in Table 3–1. The first column of the table compares U.S. exports and imports of goods, a minus sign designating an excess of imports over exports. The onset of a trade deficit in 1971 contributed to the panic that led to the first devaluation of the dollar. And the rise in the trade deficit in 1972, despite the first devaluation, forced a further depreciation of the dollar.

Table 3-1

U.S. Balance of Payments: Goods and Services

	Balance on Merchandise Trade (1)	Balance on Goods and Services (2)
	Billions of Dollars	
1970	2.6	2.9
1971	−2.3	−0.3
1972	−6.4	−6.0
1973	0.9	3.9
1974	−5.4	3.6
1975	9.0	16.3
1976	−9.3	3.6
1977 (First half on annual basis)	−29.9	−12.7

Source: 1970–1975, data from *Economic Report of the President,* January 1977; 1976 and 1977 data from *Survey of Current Business,* September 1977.

Since then, however, the trade balance seemed to be approaching some sort of equilibrium, with alternating years of surplus and deficit—until 1977. The incredibly large 1977 deficit, and the likelihood that it will be followed by a big deficit again this year, highlights a new departure in trade relations between the United States, its major trading partners, and the oil-producing countries.

The problem can be seen in better perspective from the balance-of-payments data for both goods and services shown in column 2. The net U.S. income from services, which includes as its largest component the flow of profits and fees to U.S. corporations from foreign investments, pays for a good part of the deficit arising from merchandise trade, and in some years is large enough to turn a deficit into a surplus. Still, large as the surplus on services has been, it was not big enough to prevent a whopping overall deficit in 1977, more than twice that of the previous critical year of 1972.

Nor is this by any means the whole story. For the rising deficits in the goods-and-services part of the balance of payments has not

Table 3-2
U.S. Liquid Liabilities to Foreigners[a]

End of Period	Outstanding Liabilities (Billions of Dollars)		
	Total	Average Annual Increase	
1960	21.0		
1965	29.6	1960–1965	1.7
1970	47.0	1965–1970	3.5
1971	67.8		
1972	82.9		
1973	92.5	1970–1973	15.2
1974	119.2		
1975	126.6		
1976	151.4		
1977 (Sept.)	174.2	1973–1977	20.4

(a)   Dollar deposits and short-term U.S. government securities owned by foreign
       official institutions, banks, corporations, and individuals.
Source: Federal Reserve Bulletin, various issues.

slowed down, let alone halted, the flow of dollars abroad for other purposes—"aid" to control and influence Third World countries; foreign investment by private capital; and overseas loans by U.S. banks.

Now it should be clear that any lesser power confronted with the kind of deficit shown for 1977 in Table 3-1, and facing a continuation of deficits in the year ahead, would not only be unable to engage in the export of capital but would be confronted with all-out pressure by its creditors to get its financial house in order, at the very least to balance the government budget, reduce welfare spending, and restrict consumption. How then does the United States get away with it? The answer is very simple. The United States blithely keeps on adding to the float of dollars abroad, and in effect tells the rest of the capitalist world that it can either like it or lump it. The resulting pile-up of dollars outside the United States is shown in Table 3-2. These figures represent dollars owned by foreign official institutions, banks, corporations, and individuals, which have grown primarily out of the long history of deficits in the U.S. balance of payments, the many years during which the United States spent more abroad than it earned in foreign money. The sum of $21 billion shown in Table 3-2 for 1960 was relatively modest, considering that the U.S. Treasury then had some $19 billion in the form of gold and reserves at the IMF. But since then the reserve assets of the United States have not increased a whit, while the outstanding dollar liabilities to foreigners grew at an accelerating rate to reach $174 billion by September 1977.

This ever-growing mass of U.S. dollars weighs heavily on the policies of the other capitalist nations. In a very real sense the existing international monetary system confers on the United States a much greater degree of flexibility than any of the other leading capitalist countries can command. By continuing to accept and live with this pile-up of dollars, the European and Japanese economies are in effect paying for the U.S. deficits and thus for a good part of the high American standard of living. And this generates a sort of schizophrenia among the central bankers of Western Europe and Japan. On the one hand, they are fearful that the accumulation at an accelerated rate of overseas dollars may some day topple the international financial system and thereby bring down the accompanying intricate world credit and trade structures. On the other hand, they want the international value of the U.S. dollar to remain relatively firm, for two compelling reasons: first, to prevent the dollars they own from shrinking; and second, to avoid the weakening in their own competitive position in exporting to the United States (and to third markets) which, as explained above, results from a cheaper dollar.

In contrast, the United States continues to operate as if it holds all the aces. Government representatives run around the world instructing other countries, big and small, how they should adjust their affairs to meet U.S. needs. A *Wall Street Journal* story (December 12) reports: "Recent talks by U.S. officials in Japan have been low key. However, accounts in the Japanese press, presumably based on conversations with Japanese officials, have portrayed U.S. negotiators as arm-twisting bullies."

Furthermore, the present Democratic administration pursues the same policies as its Republican predecessors. Despite all sorts of gentlemen's agreements promising to uphold the value of the dollar, Washington carries on with a policy of "benign neglect." The Americans innocently watch the dollar price sink in the foreign currency markets, trusting that this will improve the competitive position of U.S. exports and thus achieve a better balance-of-payments picture. And even though President Carter recently announced a shift to an active defense of the dollar, there is still no evidence of any basic change from "benign neglect." The truth is that realignments in trading relations and U.S. spending and lending practices abroad depend on much more than attempts to manipulate foreign currency markets.

It is against the background of this impasse, arising from heightening inter-imperialist rivalries and U.S. attempts to maintain its increasingly shaky hegemonic position, that the growth of protectionism is taking shape. Countries that have become increasingly dependent on exports but are now confronted with stagnating foreign trade are inhibited from undertaking active currency devaluations, naturally turn to behind-the-scenes trade manipulations, cartel arrangements, and overt building of trade barriers. It is too soon to tell how far or how fast protectionism will develop, or whether it will eventually lead to a fragmentation of world trade into a new system of trade and currency blocs. One thing seems clear, however: those Third World countries that are counting for salvation on an expansion of industrial exports to the advanced capitalist world are doomed to disappointment.

4.
The Present Stage of the Global Crisis of Capitalism

> The issue is the economic crisis—*la crise*. The phrase is omnipresent in political speech. By it are understood several things: high and persisting levels of unemployment and inflation; the sense that the economic boom of the postwar epoch is over; the knowledge that the economic policies of the boom can no longer ensure full employment.
>
> —Emma Rothschild, just returned from France, *New York Times*, Op-Ed page, March 1, 1978

The present economic situation in the world capitalist system is unique in so many ways that it can without doubt be called unprecedented. This is not to say that as a recession or depression it is "worse" than the Great Depression of the 1930s, only that it displays so many novel features—like the coexistence of severe unemployment and inflation—that comparisons with the past can be made only with caution and awareness of the possibility of their being as misleading as they are helpful. It is the more important to point this out because what follows deals almost exclusively with the industrialized countries of the "center," while some of the most strikingly new aspects of the present situation relate to the underdeveloped "periphery" and to center/

This is the latest version of an updated lecture delivered at the Metropolitan University, Mexico City, in January 1978, and at the University of Puerto Rico, Río Piedras, in March 1978. It originally appeared in the April 1978 issue of *Monthly Review*.

periphery relations. My excuse for this one-sided emphasis is partly lack of time, but even more that what happens throughout the whole system is crucially dependent on forces which originate in the center.*

I want to start with what I think is a very useful visual "picture" of the situation in the advanced industrial countries, i.e., a series of charts prepared by the Organization of Economic Cooperation and Development (OECD), a Paris-based "club" to which all the countries of the center belong (see pp. 50–51). All charts relate to individual countries, and they are all constructed on the same basis. The line at 1.00 represents that country's average post-Second World War rate of growth of industrial production (6 percent for France, 4.5 percent for the United States, 3 percent for Great Britain, etc.). Deviations above and below this line indicate years of faster or slower growth. The "normal" expectation of course is that growth will be below average in recessions and above average in periods of recovery, and that indeed is what the charts show for the years before 1974.

This changes dramatically in 1974. We have drawn a heavy line between 1973 and 1974; to the right of it are the years 1974, 1975, 1976, and the first three quarters of 1977—practically four full years. Look at this portion of the various charts, and you will see that 1974 and early 1975 was a period of sharp decline relative to the long-run growth rate. Recovery begins for most of the countries around the middle of 1975, a normal business-cycle pattern, and continues through 1976 and into 1977. But then an odd thing happens. With two exceptions, the United States and Italy, the recovery does not bring the growth rate up to the long-run average, and for most of the countries the line appears to be flattening out in the course of 1977 and looks very much as though it were about to turn down again, *still well below the long-run average*. The Italian case is unique in that it is the only one where the growth rate rose above the average by the end of 1976. This spurt, however, was brief, and the decline during 1977 was much sharper than in most of the other countries where the curve began to turn down in that year. Only in the United States did the

---

*For more on developments in the periphery see Chapter 5 of this volume.

curve go above the average in 1977 and remain there during the year. Of all the OECD countries, therefore, the United States stands out as a genuine exception, a subject to which we shall return presently.

In one sense what we have in these charts is obviously a picture of a cyclical decline and recovery of a kind which has always characterized the behavior of capitalism. But it is clearly much more than that. The normal pattern from past experience would be recovery from below average at the trough to above average at the succeeding peak. But here we see the apparent beginnings of a new decline with the growth rate still well below the long-term average. This is totally new in the post-Second World War period. Nothing like it has happened since the 1930s.

The consequences of this marked retardation of the growth rate have been numerous and varied. Here I will mention only the following:

(1) A growth in employment slower than in the size of the labor force. By the end of 1977 there were some 17 million officially counted unemployed workers in the OECD countries (the real figure, as in the United States, is undoubtedly much higher).

(2) A rise in idle productive capacity. In industry after industry operating rates—i.e., the percentage of productive capacity in actual use—have declined. This has been most marked in that most basic of all industries, steel. A dispatch in the *New York Times* of last May 23rd states: "From Lancashire in Britain through Belgium and the French Lorraine to the German industrial heartland of the Ruhr, Europe's steelmakers are now experiencing the worst crisis in living memory." And later in the same story we read, "Japan alone now has idle plants capable of turning out 30 million tons of steel a year, or nearly a quarter of Common Market production." In the United States, during a period of economic recovery when an expansion of steel-making capacity would be normal, the steel giants have actually been closing down plants, the most publicized case being that of Youngstown, Ohio. Or take ship-building, an outstanding contributor to the whole postwar wave of prosperity. A front-page dispatch in the *New York Times* of March 6, 1978, begins: "Shipping industries in Western industrial nations and Japan are in deep trouble, caught by a

INDUSTRIAL PRODUCTION
Deviation from long-term trend

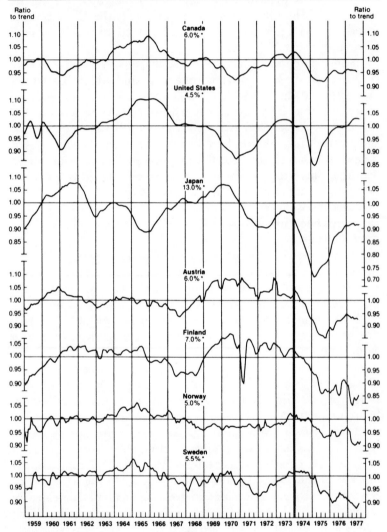

Ratio to trend

Canada 6.0% *

United States 4.5% *

Japan 13.0% *

Austria 6.0% *

Finland 7.0% *

Norway 5.0% *

Sweden 5.5% *

1959 1960 1961 1962 1963 1964 1965 1966 1967 1968 1969 1970 1971 1972 1973 1974 1975 1976 1977

*Average annual trend growth rate

Source: OECD, *Main Economic Indicators*, December 1977.

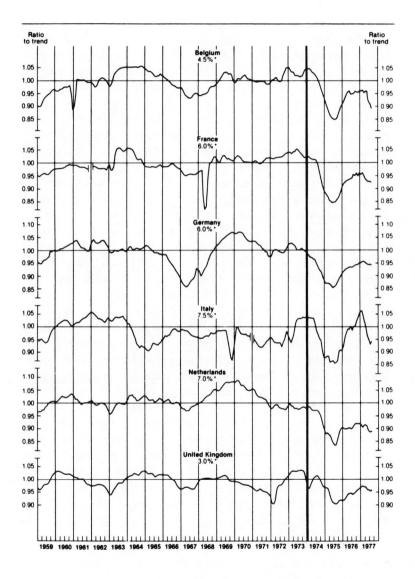

lingering glut in global capacity that has idled a third of the world's tanker tonnage and cut the ship-building business in half." But while steel and ship-building are perhaps the most dramatic examples of worldwide excess capacity, they are by no means alone. Similar stories could be told of automobiles, heavy chemicals, paper, and many more.

(3) With existing capacity seriously underutilized in so many important industries, capitalists are naturally extremely reluctant to invest in new plant and equipment, as they did so freely during the prosperous 1950s and 1960s.

Retarded growth, rising unemployment, increasing amounts of idle productive capacity, lower levels of investment in plant and equipment—these of course all act on each other as cause and effect. But they do not, individually or in combination, constitute an explanation of the situation in which the developed capitalist world now finds itself. We shall come to the problem of explanation presently. But before we do that, a few words about the exceptional case of the United States are in order.

First, the line on the U.S. chart, while differing from the others in being above 1.00 in 1977, is still below what one would expect on the basis of earlier postwar experience: an increase in the rate of industrial production to around 3 percent above the long-run average in the third year of cyclical upswing is a pretty poor showing. And even this is based on special circumstances. By far the leading factor in the U.S. recovery has *not* been, as would normally be expected, capital accumulation, but consumption. As an indication of this dominance of consumption, we may note that between 1973 and 1977 personal consumption expenditures (in constant 1972 dollars) increased by 10.8 percent, while non-residential fixed investment (also in 1972 dollars) actually *declined* by 3 percent.* And the growth of consumption has been fueled by an extraordinary explosion of consumer credit (during the years

---

Economic Indicators, Joint Economic Committee, January 1978, p. 2. I omit from consideration here other differences between the United States and the rest of the developed capitalist world—e.g., the continuing huge deficits in the federal budget, and in the last couple of years the very large and growing excess of imports over exports. In any full treatment these (and other) factors would have to be analyzed and accorded their due weight.

1970–1975 the annual net addition to consumer instalment credit outstanding averaged $11.1 billion, while in 1976 the figure rose to $20.2 billion and in 1977 to $30.9 billion*). Nor is instalment credit the only factor at work here. Homeowners in increasing numbers have been re-mortgaging their houses to take advantage of inflated real estate prices and spending the proceeds on all manner of consumer goods. Had it not been for this debt-based ballooning of consumption, there is no doubt that the performance of the U.S. economy would have been no more impressive than that of the other advanced capitalist countries. (Why this difference between the United States and the others should exist is an interesting question which I have not seen discussed in any of the relevant literature. My guess is that the reason is to be found in the longer history of consumer credit in the United States—linked to the earlier "automobilization" of U.S. society— and the more highly developed institutional mechanisms for promoting and supplying it.)

How do the establishment economists—in the universities, business, and government—explain this crisis which set in in 1974 and is now into its fifth year? In general, I think it is correct to say that most of them attribute it to a failure of government polcies. What they believe would have been the right policies of course differs from one to another. Some think that an appropriate monetary policy would have avoided the crisis, others that fiscal policy holds the key. Many combine the two—monetary and fiscal policies. But on the whole they do not seem to believe, or even suspect, that the causes lie deeper in the structure of the capitalist system where they remain immune to manipulation or correction by methods made familiar by Keynes and his followers since the 1930s, and more recently by the monetarists, of whom Milton Friedman is the best known theorist.

I have to add, however, that bourgeois thought about the crisis is not only that of professional economists. There are others, less captivated or crippled by their formal training, who are beginning to see the situation in a different light. Here I will cite only one example, a striking one, that of Jay Forrester, a computer special-

---

Ibid., p. 27.

ist and professor of management at the Massachusetts Institute of Technology, who became famous a few years ago as one of the main authors of a widely publicized work, *The Limits of Growth,* sponsored by the eminently respectable (and bourgeois) Club of Rome. In the January 16th issue of *Fortune* magazine there is an interview with Forrester under the title, "We Are Headed for Another Depression" (the context makes clear that he has in mind an experience similar to the Great Depression of the 1930s). Forrester has discovered the theory put forward in the early 1920s by the Russian economist Kondratieff who believed that capitalist history has been characterized by long cycles of some 50 years duration. That waves of accelerated and retarded growth exist is scarcely open to question, though whether they have the cyclical character attributed to them by Kondratieff is another matter, and in my view one which is not only of little importance but which can all too easily become a red herring. In the course of the interview, Forrester is quoted as saying, "The long wave is a process in which the capital-goods sectors grow to a size that cannot be sustained and then collapse."

This is clearly a very apt description of what has actually happened in the 1970s, and as such it is a good deal more enlightening than anything emanating from the professional economists, most of whom are still waiting for—and perhaps even expecting— a new boom in the capital-goods industries to put the economy on a sustained upward path again. But Forrester is no better than the economists in telling us *why* the capitalist system should behave in this fashion. And here we have to take leave of the realm of bourgeois thought entirely and seek answers in the Marxian analysis of capitalism.

The clue is to be found in understanding the nature of capital itself. Capital is not a thing, nor a sum of money, nor even only a social relation—though it partakes of all these. It is above all *self-expanding value.* In order to explain this—an idea, incidentally, which is totally foreign to all schools of bourgeois thought— we follow the notational language used by Marx in Part II of the first volume of *Capital* (entitled "The Transformation of Money into Capital"). We can imagine a society (which never existed in pure form) in which all production is by independent producers working on their own and selling what they produce to get the money to buy what they need. Each one produces a commodity C, sells it for money M, and buys other commodities which are also denoted by C. Circulation then takes the form C-M-C. In terms of exchange value the C at the beginning and the C at the end are equal, but their use value is different (for the farmer, for example, the C at the beginning stands for grain and the C at the end for the whole basket of goods he needs to sustain the life of his family). The rationale of the operation is clear: production takes place in order to satisfy the needs of the producers. This does not, however, describe what happens under capitalism where production is initiated, organized, and controlled not by independent producers, but by capitalists who begin with money M, purchase means of production and labor power C (both are commodities under capitalism), and sell the product once again for money M. Here the circulation form is M-C-M. Since money is perfectly homogeneous and directly satisfies no needs, it follows that the M at the beginning and the M at the end can be distinguished only by their magnitude. If they are quantitatively equal, the operation is meaningless. Capitalism therefore can exist only if there is some way that capitalists can regularly sell their products for more money than they had to lay out to produce them. How and why this is indeed possible is of course explained by the theory of surplus value, which for present purposes we can simply take for granted. This being so, we can formulate the circulation process under capitalism as M-C-M', where M' is greater than M. This, however, represents only one production period. At the beginning of the second period the capitalist has more money than he had at the beginning of the first. Perhaps he will want to consume more than he did before, but basically the capitalist is interested not in consumption but in production, so we can abstract from this and assume that he begins the second period with M' and emerges from it with M'' (which in turn is larger than M'). And so on and on, with the Ms getting always larger and larger.

This is what is meant by capital as self-expanding value. The capitalist is, so to speak, its agent and functionary: by the nature of the position he occupies in production and society, he must always seek to expand the capital under his control. As Marx said,

"Accumulate, accumulate, that is Moses and the prophets." The capitalist follows this imperative by maximizing the surplus value he squeezes out of the workers, and by investing in additional production as much as possible of the surplus value thus appropriated. The result is a double tendency: to accelerate society's power to produce while at the same time restraining its capacity to consume. The coexistence of tendencies to unlimited production and restricted consumption is a contradiction of the most profound kind. It is what prompted Marx to write:

> *The real barrier of capitalist production is capital itself.* It is the fact that capital and its self-expansion appear as the starting and closing point, as the motive and aim of production; that production is merely production for *capital,* and not vice versa, the means of production mere means for an ever expanding system of the life process for the benefit of the *society* of producers. *(Capital,* Kerr, ed., vol. 3, p. 293)

You might perhaps object that this theory purports to prove too much—not that capitalism is prone to crises, but that capitalism is impossible. But here we need to understand the difference between tendencies and what actually happens. Tendencies can be counteracted for shorter or longer periods of time, though if they are fundamental and inherent they sooner or later exert their dominance. The law of gravity is an apt example: if it were always operative in its pure form, there would be no such thing as an airplane. But no airplane can fly forever: sooner or later the law of gravity has its way. And so it is with the underlying tendencies of capitalism.

In certain historical contexts, capitalism's drive to unlimited expansion of production can operate freely and with only occasional or minor setbacks. Such was the case in the nineteenth century with the industrial revolution and the opening up of new continents as the context. Such is the case in major wars and the periods following major wars when so much that has been destroyed needs to be restored, and radically new relations between the various units that make up the global system are being shaped and organized. But these periods do not last forever. Gradually the underlying contradiction between the tendencies to unlimited expansion of production and restricted consumption exerts itself. And when it takes over, it assumes the form which it is the merit of Jay Forrester to have described—the capital-goods sectors are discovered to have grown to a size that cannot be sustained and their collapse follows, with dire consequences for the functioning of the entire system.*

Let me now attempt to summarize: The period beginning with the Second World War was extraordinarily favorable to the rapid expansion of production. This period lasted for three full decades—the forties, fifties, and sixties. The crisis set in in 1974 and has been with us since then. The outlook is for a new period of depression reminiscent of the thirties (some prefer to call it stagnation). How long is will last can in no way be predicted. That depends not at all on the kinds of government policies the economists think in terms of, but on whether a new historical conjuncture will take shape favorable to a resumption of the rapid expansion of production and capital accumulation. Obviously, no one can say that this will not happen, but I think one is safe in saying that the nature and outlines of such a new historical conjuncture are not now visible.

As to the implications of the present crisis, I want only to say in closing that in rejecting the fashionable view that changed economic policies will somehow turn things around, I do not mean to imply that upheavals and structural changes, either within the framework of capitalism or going beyond capitalism, are not

---

*In Marxian terms this could be reformulated to say that in periods specially favorable to the expansion of production, Department I (producing means of production) grows at an unsustainably rapid rate relative to the growth of Department II (producing consumption goods). What needs to be understood is that when the favorable conditions change and the expansion of Department I slows down, a self-reinforcing process goes into effect. This is because during the expansion of Department I, a large part of its production is plowed back into Department I itself. An analogy with the steel industry may help here. When the steel industry is growing, a lot of steel is used in the construction of new mills. When the process of expansion stops, this part of the demand for steel simply disappears, and steel-making capacity is suddenly seen to be greater than is needed to meet the requirements of the rest of the economy. But exactly the same holds for Department I as a whole since, as in the case of steel, its products are necessary for its own self-expansion. For this reason the collapse of the boom in the capital-goods sector can take place without any prior retardation, let alone cessation, of the growth of the consumption-goods sector (Department II).

possible, nor that they may not be vital aspects of a new historical conjuncture which would necessitate a drastic reappraisal of the prospects before us. We must guard against falling into rigidly determinist ways of thinking. But at the very least I believe we can assert with confidence that the crisis of the 1970s marks a crucial historical turning point, and that nothing short of very basic changes will suffice to put us on a new road.

5.
The Limits of International Reform

Even the best of reform movements tend to foster illusions. And the proposed New International Economic Order is no exception. Justifiably dissatisfied with the traditional international economic order and the practices of the imperialist powers, the leaders of the Third World have been energetically pressuring for a New Deal—one which its advocates hope and expect will eventually result in a more equitable distribution of wealth between rich and poor countries. The very unification of Third World nations around a common program—and especially one that recognizes a basic conflict of interest between the center and periphery—is undoubtedly an important step forward and may even mark the beginning of a new phase in the history of imperialism. At the same time, the rationalization and rhetoric advanced in promoting the program raise false hopes about what can in fact be accomplished within the framework of the imperialist system.

The ideas incorporated in the slogan of a New International Economic Order took shape over a roughly twenty-year period of political struggle by Third World nations to overcome what appeared to them to be the most obvious obstacles to their economic growth. It did not take long for the newly decolonized nations to become aware that political independence did not automatically remove the shackles of imperialism. And in one way or another they, together with the older politically independent nations of

This is a revised version of a talk given at the Metropolitan University, Mexico City, in January 1978, and at Columbia University in March 1978. It originally appeared in the May 1978 issue of *Monthly Review*.

the periphery, have been seeking ways to unite and exert pressure for the redress of their grievances.

The first such move took place in 1955, when twenty-nine nations sent representatives to the Asian-African Conference held in Bandung, Indonesia. There, among other matters, the participants raised one of the key demands for the economic self-defense of the periphery, calling for measures that would eliminate the wide fluctuations in income derived from the export of primary products to metropolitan centers. The significance of that conference, however, went far beyond the drafting of specific proposals for reform, for it was there that the principle of the unity of Third World interests in opposition to those of the imperialist centers began to emerge. This conference was, in effect, a prelude to various other attempts to establish a political, and eventually economic, power base that would act independently of, and wrest concessions from, the metropoles.

Additional demands for changes in the existing international political and economic arrangements were generated at several heads-of-state summit conferences of "Non-Aligned Powers," starting with an initial meeting at Belgrade in 1961. Furthermore, the four United Nations Conferences on Trade and Development, beginning with the UNCTAD I gathering in Geneva in 1964, became important forums (and only forums) at which Third World representatives (2,000 delegates from 139 countries attended UNCTAD IV) spelled out their grievances and formulated demands for changes in imperialist practices in a selected number of areas on which a consensus could be reached.

While all these assorted activities fostered an increasingly clear and more integrated Third World ideology, they also intensified the sense of frustration. Meaningful concessions from the imperialist centers simply were not forthcoming, despite all the sound and fury, and despite the potential political power of a united Third World bloc. For all intents and purposes the metropoles turned a deaf ear to the demands of the periphery.

Two developments, however, forced the rulers of the imperialist centers at least to sit up, listen, and pay lip service to the need for reforms. The first of these was OPEC's success in achieving a major hike in oil prices in 1973. And the second was the change in voting strength at the United Nations. By the early 1970s, the number of Third World members of the UN had expanded to over 110. This voting bloc—supported by the USSR, Eastern European countries, the People's Republic of China, and Scandinavian countries—could constitute a majority on many subjects of interest to the Third World. No longer able to fob off consideration of the demands for reform to subordinate debating forums, the UN General Assembly itself finally acted on the matter. The 1974 Sixth Special Session of the UN General Assembly adopted a *Declaration and Programme of Action on the Establishment of a New Economic Order,* which was designed to "work *urgently* for the establishment of a new international economic order . . . which shall correct inequalities, redress existing injustices, and make it possible to eliminate the widening gap between the developed and developing countries. . . ." This was followed by formal acceptance of a *Charter of Economic Rights and Duties of States.**

Yet, despite the vigorous program of action called for by these documents, the four years since their adoption have produced little in addition to still more conferences and ceaseless controversy on how to put the UN's resolutions into practice. The reason for this is simple enough. Each of the major items on the agenda—reduction of barriers to imports of manufactured goods from the underdeveloped countries, stabilization of income from exports of primary commodities, greater control by recipients over the transfer of technology, and debt relief (including, when necessary, debt moratoriums)—ultimately impinges on the profits accruing to the advanced capitalist nations. Not surprisingly, therefore, the imperialist centers, forced to enter into negotiations, have been playing a game of sabotage that takes one of two forms: (1) outright refusal to institute the proposed reforms, and (2) advocacy of counterproposals that either are mere window-dressing or are designed to meet their own needs, such as obtaining more secure flows of raw materials from the Third World.

These difficulties do not seem to have seriously disheartened

---

*A valuable summary and analysis of this history can be found in Orlando Letelier and Michael Moffitt, *The New International Economic Order (Part I)* (Washington, D.C.: Transnational Institute, 1977).

the leaders of the periphery. For them the hoped-for New International Economic Order remains the reigning ideology and the focal point of their collective efforts on the international scene. And here it is important to recognize that the persistence of the vision, in face of the meager results which have been achieved, is itself a reflection of the imperialist snare in which they are perforce caught. This entrapment, in ideology as well as in fact, is rooted in the great extent to which their economic survival, not to mention progress, depends on the prosperity of the metropoles, or, to put it more concretely, on how much of their exports the metropoles will buy. This crucial reliance on external demand holds true even for those Third World countries that have adopted the boldest internal-reform measures, including extensive state intervention in investment decisions. It follows that in the absence of a strategy aimed to burst asunder the traditional mold imposed by the long history of capitalism, the peripheral nations remain, willy-nilly, cogs in the imperialist machine. And regardless of how aware they are of the constraints imposed by the imperialist ties, they are confined to bargaining for concessions, no matter how dim the prospects of success.

Those who have faith in the feasibility and efficacy of a New International Economic Order naturally reject this point of view. They are convinced that the removal of some of the external obstacles to growth will at least open the door to the development of self-reliant, independent capitalist economies resembling those of the advanced capitalist nations. At the heart of this position is the theoretical perspective, openly stated or tacitly assumed, that there are clear-cut, universal laws of capitalist evolution that apply equally to *any* country that chooses the capitalist road.

Now it is true that one can make a meaningful abstraction of evolutionary stages through which the advanced capitalisms of Western Europe, the United States, and Japan have advanced. Examination of this evolution, however, reveals that the conditions which have been basic to the achievement of these successful capitalisms are diametrically *opposite* to those of the peripheral countries today. And it is precisely these differences that raise serious doubts about the ability of the peripheral countries to duplicate in any meaningful way the evolutionary stages of the developed, self-reliant nations.

A full analysis of these differences cannot be undertaken here. Those interested in pursuing this theme would do well to consult Samir Amin's *Unequal Development* (Monthly Review Press, 1976) and his article "Self-Reliance and the New International Economic Order" (*Monthly Review,* July-August 1977). For present purposes we will merely note some of the key features of the developed capitalist nations that are most relevant in highlighting the contrast between the core and the periphery.

(1) The industrial revolution, in the countries of its origin, was *preceded* by an agricultural revolution. Traditional low and unreliable yields of food and raw materials had for many centuries severely circumscribed the possibilities of economic growth. It was only after widespread and fairly rapid advances in agricultural practices enlarged the surplus of food produced in Western Europe that the threat of periodic famines was overcome, and therewith a roadblock to economic advance was removed and the conditions were created for an expanding market for both consumer goods and capital goods (initially primarily for agriculture).*

(2) Typically, the spread of the industrial revolution involved extensive "borrowing" of technology. But the successful borrowers were those who did so mainly on their own terms, generating a large domestic supply of craftsmen and technicians, and actively participating in indigenous technological advances.

(3) Continuous revolution in productive forces made possible persistent increases in productivity and an ever larger mass of surplus value, which in turn gave a great impetus to the accumulation of capital and the growth of internal markets. The requirements of advanced technology and urbanization, among other factors, increased the value of labor power and hence set the stage for a rise in real wages. It is important to understand that although the exploitation of the Third World has been an essential component of the prosperity of the core countries and that ex-

---

*See Paul Bairoch, "Agriculture and the Industrial Revolution, 1700–1914," in Carlo M. Cipolla, ed., *The Industrial Revolution* (London: Fontana/Collins, 1973).

port trade has been a crucial stimulus, the indispensable basis for the industrial growth of the successful capitalisms has been the ability to extend their *internal* markets.

(4) Underlying the revolutionizing of the productive forces was the growth of a capacity to manufacture a wide range of capital goods as well as mass consumption goods. The development of a machine-building industry contributed a high degree of flexibility in coping with rapidly changing opportunities in internal and external markets; and the expansion of production-equipment industries was itself an important source of accelerating employment and hence consumer demand.

(5) In each of the developed capitalisms an integrated and strong nation state evolved, one that was devoted primarily to the support of industrial capitalism and its allies in finance and trade. The state actively supported and assisted in the mobilization of internal resources for capital accumulation. Equally important, its foreign policy was instrumental in shaping the world capitalist system which became divided between, on the one hand, a small group of advanced capitalist countries and, on the other hand, a large number of peripheral countries subordinated to, and serving the needs of, the metropoles.

Now let us compare what has just been described with present-day conditions in the peripheral countries. There, for the most part, the agricultural revolution has still not taken place. Although high productivity has been attained in some export crops, the yield of most food crops remains incredibly low. As a result, the internal demand for more consumption goods remains relatively small: low agricultural productivity keeps a lid on farmers' ability to purchase industrial goods, and the small and unreliable surplus of food acts to depress real wages. Agricultural reforms, even those involving an honest redistribution of land, have not succeeded in removing the most important obstacles to agricultural growth. The reason for this is that the creation of a new class of small landowners by itself does little or nothing to mitigate the oppression of the farm population by larger landowners, merchants, and money-lenders.

In essence, what distinguishes the periphery's history to this day is that the engine of growth has been its exports to the metropoles. As a consequence, resources are allocated and infrastructure is constructed primarily in response to the demand emanating from the advanced capitalist countries, and only secondarily to that generated by internal markets. This type of economic growth does increase a certain kind of internal demand, but this is generally for luxury goods bought by the middle and upper classes. The backwardness of agriculture, depressed wage levels, and the persistence of mass unemployment stunt the growth of the markets for mass consumer goods.

Against this background, the potentials for self-sustaining industrialization are necessarily restricted. This has been clearly demonstrated by the experience of those underdeveloped countries which have taken initial steps looking to the achievement of greater independence and self-reliance. These efforts have all assumed the form which has come to be known as "import substitution," i.e., the establishment of a domestic manufacturing capacity to replace imported consumer goods. The limits of this strategy quickly became evident, in part because it did little to enlarge narrow internal markets. Even more important, it turned out that reliance on imports and the resulting strains on the balance of payments were not significantly eased: intermediate components, capital equipment, and in some cases raw materials, had to be obtained abroad. More recently, the shortcomings of this strategy, together with continued difficulties associated with traditional exports, have led to an alternative program for development: concentration on manufacturing industries geared to exports. And here we come full circle, for it is precisely the barrier to the sales of such products in the developed countries that has been adding pressure to the campaign for a New International Economic Order.

An additional factor of outstanding significance in frustrating the various attempts by the periphery to industrialize is the extent to which success remains dependent on the import of finance and technology from the West. To a greater or lesser extent, the Third World nations have failed to generate a population of craftspeople and technicians of the sort that enabled the developed countries to become masters of their own industrial revolution.* Nor have the Third World countries been able to create an indigenous capital-goods sector of a kind that would complement mass consumer-goods industries; in the few cases where progress has been made in machine-building, it has been confined to facilitating the manufacture of non-essential luxury goods and military equipment.

Finally, the peripheral countries—unlike the metropoles—have not succeeded in developing states that are single-mindedly devoted to developing and supporting a native independent capitalism. In general, the ruling power in these countries consists of class alliances in which groups tied to foreign investment activities are prominently represented. But even when the influence of the latter is absent from the top, the underlying dependency relationships tend to reassert themselves. For as long as the essentials of the traditional economic structure remain in force and the instability-producing influences prevail, the options for basic change are strictly limited. Any one of the recurrent crises inherent in the export-oriented economies—a critical balance-of-payments problem, a crop failure, inability to settle outstanding foreign debt—brings even the most independence-striving and determinedly reformist ruling group back into the dependency fold, seeking relief through more foreign investment or new sources of borrowing abroad.

If one examines the proposed New International Economic Order in light of these considerations, it is clear that the reforms which it embodies skirt the major issues. This can be seen in each of the four key areas under consideration.

(1) *Agriculture.* The advocated changes are concerned primarily with stabilizing and, where feasible, raising the income derived from agriculture (and mineral) exports. Wide fluctuations in income and adverse terms of trade do of course create serious problems for the periphery. But it is important to recognize that

---

*Some of the Third World countries, like India and China, have a long history of fine craftsmanship. Much of this (though not all) was destroyed in the heydey of imperialist expansion, when they were inundated by cheap manufactured goods from the industrializing center. To start over again without first withdrawing from the imperialist framework has proved impossibly difficult.

these proposals have nothing to do with the more fundamental constraints in the field of agriculture, which arise from inferior productivity in food crops and internal social obstacles to the expansion of the food supply.

(2) *Exports of manufactures.* The main emphasis here is on the removal of trade barriers and obtaining especially favorable opportunities to penetrate the markets of the industrialized countries. Such concessions, however, would not overcome the normal competitive forces operating inside these countries. To outsell the products of metropolitan industries, the manufacturers of the periphery would have to charge consistently lower prices, an advantage that could be maintained only by keeping wages down, thus blocking the development of internal markets for mass consumer goods.

(3) *Technology transfer.* Proposed reforms under this heading have to do with improving the terms under which technology is obtained from multinational corporations. While such reforms, if obtained, might ease some of the balance-of-payment burdens, they do not attack the central issue of developing an independent technological base and an indigenous research and development capability for the generation of technology adapted to their special needs. In the final analysis, the proposed reforms would still keep the underdeveloped countries in thrall to the multinational corporations and the technology of advanced capitalism.

(4) *Debt reform.* This has to do with much-needed relief from the stranglehold of mounting foreign debt. But the various forms of relief considered, including moratoriums, deal only with surface phenomena and not with the conditions that create more or less permanent debt peonage. The debt problem arose long before the rise in oil prices; it is an age-old burden which synthesizes the whole pattern of dependency. Recurrent balance-of-payment deficits stem not only from the instability of income from exports, but more importantly from the perpetual and ever swelling outflow of funds to firms in the metropoles in payment for shipping, insurance, banking services, royalties on patents and trademarks, management fees, dividends, and interest. Important as debt relief may be in the current situation, it can only serve as a temporary palliative as long as the conditions that create the need for debt persist.

Thus far we have discussed the New International Economic Order from the angle of the Third World. But what about the advanced capitalist nations?

It is conceivable that the metropoles might in theory be inclined to make some concessions, especially those that would bring them certain long-run advantages, such as securing more reliable sources of raw materials, protecting their multinational firms from nationalization or confiscation, and building up junior partners prepared to help preserve capitalism in the Third World. These possible long-run advantages, however, are offset by real and compelling constraints in the short run. The imperialist powers have entered a new stage of stagnation.* The international money system is shaky. World trade has slowed down. Trade and currency competition among the leading powers has been intensifying. Every one of the industrialized countries is confronted with internal problems arising from persistent unemployment and weak industrial and financial sectors. These are hardly the conditions under which the imperialist powers are inclined to consider reforms that promise to intensify their internal contradictions.†

The greatest illusion permeating the arguments for the New International Economic Order is that a new division of income between the rich and poor nations in the capitalist world system can be achieved through diplomatic negotiations. The more realistic question that needs answering is entirely different: Is self-reliant development in the Third World at all possible as long as these countries remain enmeshed in the imperialist network

---

*See Chapter 4 of this volume.

†An interesting and illustrative clue to their attitudes is provided by the alarm expressed by the huge steel corporations here and abroad over the entrance into the world market of a relatively small amount of steel exports from some Third World countries. Equally noteworthy is the recent treaty between the United States and Mexico, in which the United States reduced tariffs on fruits, vegetables, and handicrafts—a group of products which in 1976 accounted for $63 million of Mexican exports to the United States. In return for this munificent gesture the United States insisted on, and obtained, trade concessions from Mexico on U.S. exports of evaporated and other milk, lard, canned fruit cocktail, electric motors, and other products! (See Clyde H. Farnsworth, "Mexico Makes Reverse Concessions in U.S. Trade Pact," *New York Times*, December 3, 1977.)

and the basic dependency relationship remains? At bottom, the true issue rests on the choice between reform under imperialism and a breakaway from imperialism. The changes advocated by the New International Economic Order, even if by some miracle they were adopted, would not overcome the impoverishment of the masses, backward agriculture, distorted industrial and economic structures subservient to the metropoles, illiteracy, inadequate education and health services, and all the other ills that beset these societies. Solutions for such problems can only arise from internal changes in class power leading to a revolutionary alteration of social priorities which elevate the interests of the masses to the paramount position.

6.
Debt and the Business Cycle

One of the most characteristic features of the business cycle is the alternating expansion and contraction of credit. During the upturn from a recession or depression, business firms need more money than is flowing into the till. They must rush to grab every emerging profit-making opportunity and to fend off competitors from encroaching on their share of the market. Money is therefore sought for a variety of needs, such as expanding capacity, filling up inventory pipelines, adding labor-saving machinery, and intensifying sales promotion. Banks, most of whose profits come from making loans, are happy to accommodate this rising demand for money. In fact financial institutions add their bit to the expansion of credit during the upswing of the cycle by stimulating new uses of debt by business and consumers.

The feverish speculation that thrives in such an environment, added to the competitive struggles among firms, pushes production beyond what can be maintained, even when account is taken of the accompanying growth of consumer income. And following the inevitable downturn in the cycle comes a contraction of credit. Some loans are wiped off the books because of business failures. But even stronger firms reduce their credit lines as they cut back operations, sell off inventories, and pull in their horns on new construction. Consumer credit of course also contracts as unemployment spreads and incomes decline. During this period of debt contraction, the sturdier banks and industrial firms get their finances into better shape, and the decks are cleared for the next upswing in borrowing.

This article originally appeared in the June 1978 issue of *Monthly Review*.

What we have been describing so far is the "normal" pattern of credit cycles. Something new, however, has been added in recent U.S. experience. With the exhaustion of the special prosperity-supporting forces of the early post-Second World War decades and the consequent onset of a period of stagnation, the U.S. economy has become *increasingly addicted to the use of debt*. The characteristic credit waves continue, but with a most significant difference: the levels of credit usage keep creeping up from one recession to another and from one peak of the business cycle to the next. More and more, the overall economic levels during both recession and recovery are sustained by greater injections of credit by both government and private agencies. The significance of this development is twofold: it reflects a weakening of the base of the hitherto high level of economic performance; and it portends growing instability.

What has been happening is shown in Table 6-1. As can be seen in the first column of the table, the total net borrowing by business, farms, banks, consumers, and governmental bodies amounted to $38.5 billion in 1960. Last year, the figure reached $378.3 billion. This almost tenfold increase is of course partly the result of inflation. A more meaningful measure of the enlarged role of credit is therefore given in the third column, where each year's increase in debt is compared with the same year's Gross National Product. Here we note that net additions to public and private debt rose from less than 8 percent of GNP in 1960 to over 18 percent in 1973. It is true that 1960 was a year when the credit cycle was in a downward phase, but even when we compare the 1973 peak (prior to the recent recession) with a preceding peak year such as 1965, we find a whopping increase of 60 percent— that is, from the 11.4 percent of GNP in 1965 to the 18.2 percent in 1973.

Striking as these changes are, they are merely a prelude to the unprecedented debt pattern of the current business cycle. The data in the third column of Table 6-1 for the period 1974–1977 show that even in the years of declining credit use, the low in 1975 (12.9 percent of GNP) was 70 percent above the figure for the recession year of 1960. Now let us look at the data for 1977—the third year of recovery from the 1974 recession. In the normal

Table 6-1
Debt and Gross National Product

	(1) Net Additions to Public and Private Debt — Billions of $ —	(2) Gross National Product	(3) Net Additions as a Percent of Gross National Product (Col. 1 ÷ Col. 2) × 100
1960	38.5	506.0	7.6%
1965	78.1	688.1	11.4
1973	238.0	1.306.6	18.2
1974	209.2	1,412.9	14.8
1975	196.5	1,528.8	12.9
1976	265.3	1,706.5	15.5
1977	378.3	1,889.6	20.0

Source: Data on debt from Board of Governors of the Federal Reserve System, *Flow of Funds Accounts 1946–1975* and *Flow of Funds Accounts 4th Quarter 1977*. Data on Gross National Product from *Survey of Current Business,* various issues.

course of events we would of course expect an increase in the use of credit during such an expanding phase of the business cycle. The whole recovery, however, was unusually feeble: the understated official rate of unemployment averaged out as much as 7 percent and capital investment remained below the preceding 1973 peak. Yet this faltering recovery was based on a new high in the use of credit, reaching 20 percent of GNP in 1977!

Significantly, the government's contribution to this ever-expanding prop to a weakening economy has been crucial. Various financial devices, such as secondary mortgage markets and intermediate credit agencies guaranteed by the federal government, have from time to time been introduced or expanded with a view to supporting and facilitating loans to private enterprise. In addition, the Federal Reserve Board has used its position as lender of last resort to back up the banks whenever they seemed in danger of getting into trouble because of excessive credit creation. And finally there has been the manipulation of the public debt itself.

As can be seen in Table 6-2, the share of the total debt ac-

Table 6-2
Public vs. Private Debt

	Net Additions to Public Debt		Net Additions to Private Debt	
	Billions of $	*Percent of Total*	*Billions of $*	*Percent of Total*
1960	4.0	10.4%	34.5	89.6%
1965	11.9	15.2	66.2	84.8
1973	41.4	17.4	196.6	82.6
1974	51.1	24.4	158.1	75.6
1975	110.1	56.0	86.4	44.0
1976	102.2	38.5	163.1	61.5
1977	107.7	28.5	270.6	71.5

Note: Data obtained from same source as given in Table 6-1. Public debt includes borrowing by state and local governments, the federal government, and U.S. government-sponsored credit agencies and mortgage pools. Private debt includes borrowing by consumers and financial and nonfinancial business firms.

counted for by government borrowing has been persistently growing. For example, in the 1974 recession it accounted for 24.4 percent as compared with 10.4 percent in the recession year of 1960. Even more striking is the enormous and unusual participation of government debt during the first year of recovery (56 percent in 1975), a complement to the very substantial contraction of the private debt that year. Yet even such an "electric shock" (a more than doubling of public debt from 1974 to 1975) was hardly adequate to keep up the momentum. But with private debt leaping forward in 1976 and 1977, economic activity did keep moving ahead, but not without continuing heavy doses of public debt only slightly below that of the peak year 1975. In other words, heavy government deficit financing has moved far beyond its "Keynesian" assignment of moderating the downward swing of the business cycle or initiating an upturn. In the present period of stagnation, government deficit financing has shown itself to be essential not only in combating the slump but also in sustaining the recovery during its entire course.

The atypical nature of the current recovery shows up not only

Table 6-3
Net Additions to Debt in Private Nonfinancial Sectors

	Consumers	Business	Consumers	Business
	— Billions of $ —		— 1973 = 100 —	
1973	78.0	87.3	100.0	100.0
1974	48.1	92.9	61.7	106.4
1975	47.5	37.4	60.9	42.8
1976	88.8	64.1	113.8	73.4
1977	130.0	103.1	166.7	118.1

Note: Data from same source as given in Table 6-1. Consumer debt includes residential mortgages and consumer credit. Business debt includes credit (other than trade credit) raised by corporations, farms, and nonfarm noncorporate firms.

in the growing reliance on government debt, but in the peculiar behavior of private debt as well. This we can observe in Table 6-3, where an impressive difference between the rise in consumer and business debt is recorded. The increase in consumer debt in 1977 was 67 percent higher than in 1973, the previous peak year; while the corresponding figure for business debt between the same two years was only 18 percent. If we adjust for the influence of inflation, however, we discover that the net new business debt in 1977 was in fact 17 percent *below* that of 1973, while the rise in real net consumer debt was 25 percent *higher*.*

The relative sluggishness in the growth of private business debt is undoubtedly a reflection of the excess capacity built up during the long postwar boom. In the third year of the recovery from the 1974 recession, manufacturing industries were still operating at only slightly above 82 percent of capacity, according to Federal Reserve Board estimates. And it is therefore not surprising to

---

*The adjustment for price changes was made by dividing the debt data by the relevant "implicit price deflators" used for the Department of Commerce's price-adjusted GNP estimates. These price figures are given in the *Survey of Current Business,* various issues. Note also that the total of consumer and business debt (columns 1 and 2) in Table 6-3 does not equal the figure for private debt in Table 6-2 (column 3). The reason is that the debt of financial institutions is included in Table 6-2 but not in Table 6-3.

Table 6-4
Consumer Debt vs. Consumer Income

	(1) *Net Additions to Consumer Debt* — *Billions of $* —	(2) *Consumer Disposable Income*	(3) *Net Additions as a Percent of Income* *(Col. 1 ÷ Col. 2) × 100*
1960	17.6	349.4	5.0%
1965	29.0	472.2	6.1
1973	78.0	901.7	8.7
1974	48.1	984.6	4.9
1975	47.5	1,084.4	4.4
1976	88.8	1,185.8	7.5
1977	130.0	1,309.2	9.9

Note: Data from same sources as given in Table 6-1. Net additions to consumer debt include residential mortgages, instalment credit, bank loans, and other forms of consumer credit. Disposable income is personal income after income taxes.

find that 1977 business investment in plant and equipment had not yet returned to the previous peak. In the light of this poor performance of capital investment, industrial production as a whole could move ahead only under the impact of a sufficiently rapid rise of consumer demand. But given the persistence of mass unemployment and the existing distribution of income, consumer demand would require a very special stimulus to be able to play this role. The answer then had to be found in a major resurgence of consumer debt in the form of instalment credit and real estate mortgages.* And that, as shown in Table 6-3, is exactly what happened. In effect, then, the current business recovery has been bought on credit—primarily by a sizable increase in consumer borrowing piled on top of persistently heavy government debt creation.

---

*The increase in mortgages is being used for more than new housing. Mortgage debt on *existing* homes tripled in less than three years, according to a *New York Times* dispatch of December 18, 1977. This means that homeowners have been adding to their mortgage debt, based on the inflated prices of residences, to help carry the load of higher prices of consumer goods and services, to repair their homes, to pay for college tuition, and to buy consumer durables.

Dependence on consumer debt for business expansion is of course not a new phenomenon. But what is new is the rapidly growing importance of this form of borrowing. As shown in Table 6-4, net additions to consumer debt increased as a percent of disposable income (that is, personal income after taxes) from 5 percent in 1960 to 8.7 percent in 1973 and then to almost 10 percent in 1977.

In part the rise in consumer debt is the result of the pressure of inflation on consumers. But one should not overlook the effects of aggressive salesmanship. A report in the *Wall Street Journal* (September 13, 1977) highlights efforts by banks to lure consumers to take out loans by offering attractive gifts to borrowers—such as electric sanders, watches, coffee-makers, and electric saws—and concludes: "Obviously times have changed in the financial world; more and more banks have become convinced that loans, like any other product, have to be marketed as aggressively as soap powder and cereal."

Even more extensive high-pressure sales campaigns have been conducted by banks to induce consumers to use automatic bank overdrafts and credit cards. Information is not available on the extent of overdraft borrowing, but we do know that instalment credit extended through the medium of bank credit cards grew from $13.9 billion in 1973 to $31.8 billion in 1977 (*Economic Indicators,* March 1978). There seems to be no end to the all-out promotion campaigns financial firms have been devising to create credit addiction. Currently, for example, Citibank is running a sweepstakes that promises 25,000 prizes to users of its credit cards; the chances of winning in the lottery increase with the number of times a card is used to make purchases.

All this ballyhoo was still not enough to overcome some major pockets of consumer resistance. The trouble was that rising interest rates and prices combined to produce monthly instalment payments higher than could be handled by otherwise potential customers. Nothing daunted, financial firms tackled this problem by stretching out the repayment schedules. Throughout the post-Second World War period the time for repayment of loans on autos (by far the largest single course of consumer credit) kept on being lengthened beyond the traditional eighteen months. By

Table 6-5
Consumer Credit and Consumer Durable Goods

	(1) Net Additions to Consumer Credit — Billions of $ —	(2) Consumer Durable Goods Purchased	(3) Consumer Credit as a Percent of Durable Goods Purchased (Col. 1 ÷ Col. 2) × 100
1973	22.0	123.7	17.8%
1974	10.2	122.0	8.4
1975	9.4	132.9	7.1
1976	23.6	158.9	14.9
1977	35.6	179.8	19.8

Note: Data from same sources as given in Table 6-1. The first column includes instalment and other consumer credit; home mortgages and general bank loans are excluded.

1974, thirty-six months became the standard maturity. But even this stretched-out repayment period proved insufficient to revive auto sales. Each year since 1974, more and more loans have exceeded the thirty-six-month standard. In 1977, 82 percent of new-car loans were for three years, with one third of the loans running for four years, and some even for five. (Based on a survey by the American Bankers Association, as reported in the *Wall Street Journal,* September 28, 1977.)

The upshot of these diverse and strenuous efforts is shown in Table 6-5, where a comparison is made between the net additions to consumer credit and annual purchases of consumer durable goods. Here we zero in on consumer debt (other than residential mortgages) which for the most part is used to finance the purchase of durable goods, notably autos. (This is of course not to deny that some of the money raised by refinancing mortgages on old residences is also used for such purchases.) The significance of the particular comparison shown in Table 6-5 is that sales of consumer durables are major contributors to the up-and-down swings of the business cycle. And here once again—despite the fact that the data in the second column of the table tend to obscure the volatility of the quantity of sales of these products

Table 6-6
Hypothetical Illustration of the
Effect of Consumer Credit on Purchasing Power

Assumptions:　1.　$90 billion of loans are extended to consumers each year.
　　　　　　　2.　These loans are repaid in three equal annual install-
　　　　　　　　　ments plus 10% interest on the outstanding balance.

Year	(1) Consumer Loans Extended	(2) 1st Year Debt	(3) 2nd Year Debt	(4) 3rd Year Debt	(5) Total Repayments	(6) Net Additions to Consumer Purchasing Power
		— Repayment on —				
		(Billions of $)			(2) + (3) + (4)	(1) − (5)
1	90	39	—	—	39	51
2	90	36	39	—	75	15
3	90	33	36	39	108	−18

owing to the influence of rising prices—we can observe the dependence of the current recovery on debt. The substantial 47
percent increase in the value of consumer durables sold between
1974 and 1977 was supported by a 249 percent rise in net additions to consumer credit from $10.2 to $35.6 billion.

In analyzing this phenomenon it is essential to keep in mind
that consumer debt in and of itself has a propensity to cyclical
behavior, and that just as it has been a factor in pushing the
economy up, it can be and usually is a factor in the downswing as
well. The simplified hypothetical illustration in Table 6-6 is designed to help explain this point.

Let us assume that there is a steady creation of $90 billion
additional consumer credit each year, that these loans have to be
paid back in three equal annual instalments at the end of each
year, and that interest charges are ten percent on the outstanding
balance. If you will look at the first line of Table 6-6, you will see
that since in the first year $90 billion is lent and $39 billion ($30
billion for repayment and $9 billion for interest) returned to the
banks, the net contribution to consumer purchasing power is $51
billion. During the second year, the repayment on the first year's
loan goes down to $36 billion, but there is also a flow-back of $39

billion on the second year's loan. Now, even though $90 billion is added to consumer purchasing power, the *net* positive stimulus to purchasing power declined from $51 billion in year one to $15 billion in year two. Following this process to its conclusion, we see that in the third year the continued creation of credit at the same rate results in an actual *reduction* of the total available consumer purchasing power.

What this example demonstrates is that steady additions to consumer credit contain the paradox that before long they will reduce instead of increase purchasing power.* The economy of course does not work so simply. The initial contribution to purchasing power generates additional production and employment, helping in this way to accelerate the economy on the way up. If there is little else to keep the recovery alive, however, the effect of this stimulus also peters out—*unless ever larger injections of credit are forthcoming.* But even this runs up against barriers, since there is a practical limit to how much consumers can pay out on instalment loans and mortgages and still meet their normal costs for food, rent, clothing, medical care, etc.

This innate cyclical nature of consumer credit is an important explanation of the extreme fluctuations shown in the first column of Table 6-5. Despite rising prices, and therefore the need for ever more credit just to keep on an even keel, net additions to consumer credit fell by almost 60 percent between 1973 and 1975. On the other hand, the sharp recovery in 1976 and 1977 provided the basis for the strong upturn in auto sales and the accompanying stimulus that a rise in auto production brings. But, as can be seen in the last column of the table, the upsurge of consumer credit was greater than the sales of consumer durables, and the contribution of consumer credit in this area in 1977 was even greater than it had been in the preceding peak year of 1973.

While there is no reliable way of forecasting precisely the course

---

*It should be noted that this paradox applies to *all* forms of private debt, though the details vary with the type of debt. In all cases the same features occur: the upward phase of the cycle is stimulated; ever larger injections of credit are needed to sustain the stimulus; at some point, because of the repayment requirements, the debt load cannot be increased sufficiently rapidly and the stimulating effect turns into the opposite; and finally, reduction in the creation of new debt intensifies the downward swing of the cycle.

of events, the foregoing analysis points to a simple conclusion. To the extent that the current recovery rests on a continuous rise in consumer spending, mainly on durable goods, an *increasing* flow of consumer credit will be needed. But we have also seen that expanding consumer credit will eventually—and sooner rather than later—turn back on itself as the stream of accompanying repayments grows inexorably larger.

One other implication of the foregoing anaylsis can stand emphasis. We called attention to the continuing importance of government deficit spending throughout the current upswing. As the time for a new recession nears—most observers of the business scene seem to think it will set in within a year at the outside—it will be interesting to see what policies the economic wizards inside and outside the government will prescribe as a way to turn things around again. With huge deficits needed even in the last year of a cyclical expansion, will they propose even larger ones to cope with the ensuing contraction? Or will they finally conclude that the jig is up and that capitalism must now at long last be allowed to go through the wringer of an old-fashioned depression of a kind they only recently thought was a thing of the past?

Time will tell. Meanwhile, as the situation becomes increasingly clear to those with eyes to see, the left has an opportunity unprecedented in the postwar period to win converts through the sheer force of convincing reason. The deepest contradictions of capitalism are surfacing in a way that has not happened since the 1930s, and the margin for reformist palliatives which existed four decades ago has been nearly used up. The manipulators and regulators of the system have had their day; the time has come to raise the banner of socialism, not as a utopia or panacea, but as a scientific explanation of the crisis of the system and the only possible way forward.

Is it necessary to add that this does *not* mean renouncing concrete struggles to wring from the ruling class what is needed to meet the urgent and in all too many cases desperate needs of tens of millions of people in the developed capitalist countries and hundreds of millions in the underdeveloped Third World? These struggles will not change the nature of capitalism, but they can force concessions and in so doing prepare the way and educate to the need for the still greater struggles that lie ahead.

7.
Corporations, the State, and Imperialism

The fact that the title for this talk was given to me by the organizers of this lecture series reflects what is doubtless a widespread conviction that corporations, the state, and imperialism are intimately interrelated both in theory and in practice. My assignment, I take it, is to attempt to throw light on the nature of these interrelations. And the most logical way to proceed is first to define the three concepts individually and then to inquire as to how they are related to each other.

(1) Corporations are the typical twentieth-century units of business enterprise—first and foremost in production but also in commerce and finance.

(2) The state is the institution which makes the laws and enforces them through an apparatus of armed force (including police), courts, prisons, etc. The state has a definite territorial identity: the area in which it operates is a nation, and within the nation's borders it is said to be "sovereign." The two characteristic features of sovereignty are a monopoly of (a) the legal use of armed force, and (b) the legal creation of money.

(3) Imperialism is the process by which the corporations and the state team up to expand their activities, their interests, and their power beyond their borders.

The essential components of the corporation are capital and labor. Capital is money and means of production *in relation to* living labor. Only in combination with living labor is capital "pro-

---

This is a reconstruction from notes of a lecture given at Stanford University in April 1978. It originally appeared in the November 1978 issue of *Monthly Review*.

ductive," i.e., only thus is a product turned out which is sufficient to sustain the laborers and leave a surplus for the owners of capital.

How does it happen that the laborers are willing to play this role? Why don't they use their own money and means of production, keep the whole product for themselves, and eliminate the capitalists altogether? The answer of course is that as the result of a long historical process reaching back into the fifteenth and sixteenth centuries, the laborers have been separated from their means of production and are obliged to sell their labor power to capitalists as the only way to avoid destitution and starvation. In other words, the means of production have been concentrated in the hands of capitalists, which today means corporations, and the workers have been transformed into wage-earners. In the United States this process was compressed into the relatively short span of two centuries. When the United States became a nation, more than three quarters of the workers were self-employed (owned their own means of production); today perhaps as many as 90 percent work for others, mostly corporations. The questions is, why do workers tolerate this state of affairs? There are of course several reasons, but the most important one which underlies all the others is the system of private property, deeply imbedded in the constitution and the laws and vigilantly enforced by the state.

Thus the corporations are completely dependent on the state for their very existence, and the state in turn lives off the surplus produced by the workers and accruing to the capitalists, which means in the first instance to the corporations. The state and the corporations thus exist in a condition of symbiosis, each deeply dependent on the other.

Coming now to the problem of imperialism, we have to ask why this symbiotic relationship between corporations and state should result in a process of expansion in which the two mutually support each other. In other words, why isn't the relationship a static one which simply reproduces itself without essential change from one period to the next? To answer this it is essential to understand the nature of a unit of capital, which is what a corporation is, in the overall capitalist economy.

Here we can call on an extremely useful pedagogical device, comparing capitalism to simple commodity production, a mode of production which never actually existed independently of other modes of production. It should be emphasized, however, that simple commodity production is in no sense an *imaginary* mode of production: its component elements have existed in many historical societies, and in some regions at certain times it has come close to realization as an integrated and coherent form (for example, in certain parts of North America in the century or so surrounding the American Revolution). The defining characteristic of simple commodity production is that producers own their own means of production and satisfy their needs through exchange with other similarly situated producers. Farmers owning their own land, implements, and animals produce more food than they need, weavers more cloth, tailors more suits, hatters more hats, shoemakers more shoes, etc. Each producer takes his surplus to market and exchanges it for money, and with the money so acquired he buys the products of the others which he requires to satisfy his family's needs. Symbolically, this process can be represented, following Marx, by the formula C–M–C where the first C stands for a specific commodity being marketed by its producer, the M for the money the producer gets in exchange, and the second C for the bundle of useful commodities which he buys with this money. Here, obviously, we are talking about a system of production for use. The link is indirect: producers do not use their own products (or at least by no means all of them), but nevertheless their purpose in producing is to satisfy their needs, not to add to their wealth. In such a society—and indeed this tends to be true of all precapitalist societies—anyone whose purpose is to amass wealth as such is looked upon as a deviant, a miser, not a rational person.*

Matters are radically different when we come to capitalism, a society in which the actual producers own no means of production, are unable to initiate a process of production, and hence must sell their labor power to capitalists who do own means of production and are therefore in control of the processes of production. Here the defining formula C–M–C loses its relevance

---

*In Webster's unabridged dictionary the first meaning given for "miser" is "a wretched or severely afflicted person."

and must be replaced by its "opposite," M–C–M. What this symbolizes is that the capitalist who is the initiator of the production process starts with money (M). With this he purchases commodities (C) consisting of means of production and labor power which he transforms through a process of production into finished commodities ready for sale. When the sale has been completed he finds himself once again with money (M): the circuit is closed.

In the C–M–C case the first and last terms can be, and indeed are normally expected to be, quantitatively equal, i.e., to have the same exchange value. The rationale of the operation lies not in the realm of exchange value but in that of use value: for the simple commodity producer the C at the end has a greater use value than the C at the beginning, and it is this increase in use value which motivates his behavior. Nothing of the sort exists in the M–C–M case. The first and last terms are both money which is qualitatively homogeneous and possesses no use value of its own. It follows that if the two Ms are also quantitatively equal, the operation totally lacks any rationale: no capitalist is going to lay out money and organize a process of production in order to end up with the same amount of money as he had at the outset. From this we can deduce that for capitalism to exist at all the M at the end must be larger than the M at the beginning. We can therefore rewrite the formula as M–C–M′ where M′ = M + △M. Here △M represents more money or, as Marx called it, more value *(Mehrwert)*, which is customarily translated into English as surplus value.*

So far we have been considering what happens in a given period, say a year: the capitalist lays out M at the beginning of the year and ends up with M′ at the end. But this is only the start of an analysis: the capitalist does not wind up his enterprise at the end of a single production cycle. The enterprise continues to operate from one cycle to the next into the indefinite future, often outliving generations of its capitalist owners. And the enterprise which had a capital of M at the beginning of the first year starts the second with M′, and this in turn becomes M″, M‴, M⁗, and so

---

*We are not concerned in the present context with the *origin* of surplus value but rather with (1) its presence as a necessary condition for the existence of capitalism, and (2) with some of its crucially important implications for the way capitalism functions.

on and on in successive years. This is what Marx meant when he defined capital as self-expanding value. Of course, not every individual unit of capital succeeds in living up to its ideal: many fall by the wayside or are gobbled up by luckier or more efficient rivals. But this only increases the importance of "trying harder," and the harder they all try the more marked becomes capitalism's essential nature as an expanding universe. Considered as a whole, capital *must* expand: the alternative is not a relaxed and happy condition of zero growth, as some liberal reformists would like to believe, but convulsive contraction and deepening crisis.

Given the symbiotic relation between the corporate units of capital and the state, it is but a logical corollary that the state is as expansion-minded as the corporations. This does not mean that the state is necessarily fixated on its own expansion; it means simply that the state's primary concern is the expansion of capital, for the very simple reason that any faltering in this respect means crisis for the whole society including, of course, the state. How this primary concern of the state is implemented, however, depends on the circumstances of time and place.

In an earlier period of capitalist history when the individual units of capital were small and capitalist relations were expanding rapidly into a precapitalist environment, the domestic tasks of the state were relatively simple: helping to create a suitable wage-labor force through direct or indirect expropriation of independent farmers and artisans; providing infrastructure in the forms of roads, canals, and railways; and maintaining a reasonably orderly monetary and financial system. In the international sphere, the main task of the state was to assure for its own producers access to external markets on the most favorable terms possible—a task which involved continuous conflict with foreign states and led to innumerable commercial and colonial wars.

But as capitalism in a given area approaches maturity—i.e., as the size of the units of capital grows, taking on the corporate form with an attendant development of monopolies and oligopolies; as the precapitalist segment of the population dwindles; and as the problems of cyclical recessions and secular stagnation become increasingly serious—as these and other factors operate to multiply and intensify the obstacles to the continued expansion of capital, the role of the state takes on new dimensions of magnitude and complexity. Many of its new or enlarged functions have to do primarily with internal matters (e.g., fiscal and monetary policies), while others are essentially international.* Here our interest is mainly in the latter.

The starting point, as always, is the conditions and requirements of the expansion of capital (I keep insisting on this because it is the *sine qua non* of *any* understanding of how capitalist societies actually work). Starting in a single industry and contributing a small share of the industry's total output, the typical unit of capital grows by accumulation, acquisition, and merger to be large relative to the industry's total output—in other words, it grows faster than the industry as a whole and as a consequence conquers an increasing degree of monopoly power. But there comes a time when this process reaches a limit. Theoretically, it could continue until one firm controlled the whole industry, but this situation is rarely reached: the normal situation is oligopoly (a few sellers) rather than monopoly (one seller), with each of the oligopolists powerful enough to hold its own against its rivals. When this stage has been reached, the conditions of further expansion are basically altered. The achievement of oligopoly status usually brings greater profitability, hence ability to accumulate more rapidly, at the same time that possibility of expansion within the industry is restricted to the rate of growth of the industry as a whole. Under these circumstances accumulation increasingly takes the form of conglomeration (expansion into other industries which have not yet reached the same degree of maturity) and multinationalization (expansion beyond existing national boundaries). It is the latter which sets new tasks for the state.

There are two kinds of multinationalization which need to be

---

*An important point which cannot be developed in the present context is that internal policies of the state often involve significant conflicts of interest within the national ruling class which under certain conditions may become so serious as to impair or even paralyze effective state action—a problem which has received far less attention than it deserves in discussions of the Marxist theory of the state. Such conflicts are much less likely to be involved in the external policies of the state; the entire national capitalist class is normally interested in maximizing gains at the expense of foreign nations and peoples.

distinguished. The first takes place within the developed core of the global capitalist system (interpenetration of each other's territory by national oligopolists), and the second takes place between the developed core countries and the underdeveloped periphery. The first kind, interpenetration, does not pose any particularly urgent problems for the state. It has taken place on a vast scale since the Second World War, with the main direction of movement being from the United States to Western Europe and, to a much smaller extent, Japan. In the last few years, however, there has been an increasing flow in the opposite directions, with European and Japanese firms setting up branches or affiliates in the United States. Since all these countries have well developed capitalist systems and stable state structures, and since they are all deterred from putting obstacles in the way of this kind of capital movement by the credible threat of retaliation, the states involved have not found it necessary or useful to adopt policies or apply measures with respect to foreign capital greatly different from those in force domestically. (This has been less true of Japan which, for historical reasons, developed its own capitalism behind an elaborate screen of protective devices. But here, too, the mutual pressures of multinationalization have been slowly prying Japan open to foreign capital: Japanese "exceptionalism" seems to be more a matter of the past than of the present or future.)

When it comes to the other kind of multinationalization, however, matters are very different. It can be said without fear of exaggeration that the expansion of capital into the underdeveloped periphery on the scale desired, and in a real sense needed, by the oligopolistic corporations of the advanced countries would be totally impossible without the massive and unremitting application of the power of their states, either individually or collectively (including through such agencies as the International Monetary Fund and the World Bank), to the shaping and maintenance of an institutional setting and what is known as an "investment climate" favorable to the functioning of profit-oriented capitalist enterprise. This application of power takes place directly (as in Greece in the 1940s, Vietnam, and the Dominican Republic; or the recent French intervention in Zaire; or a long string of CIA-organized coups in Iran, Guatemala, Greece in

1967, Bangladesh, etc.) or indirectly through arming, financing, and politically supporting client regimes throughout the Third World to repress their own people, and in some cases to act in addition as subimperialist gendarmes in their respective geographical regions. The enormous apparatus of power necessary to sustain this world-wide enterprise in geopolitical engineering is centered in the United States and benefits from important and sometimes vital support from the other advanced capitalist countries acting as junior partners; it involves the deployment of military bases with their complements of military personnel and weapons over three quarters or so of the surface of the globe; and its bitter fruit is a fearsome crop of increasingly numerous and brutal dictatorships seeking to make the world safe for capital, and in the process making it less and less habitable for human beings.

In the ideology of capitalism, of course, this very dark cloud has a silver lining. The repression, the suffering, the misery of the present are supposed to be temporary, unavoidable aspects of a transition from underdevelopment and backwardness to the promised land of full-fledged capitalism. And not surprisingly in this ideological fairy tale it is precisely the expansion of the multinational corporations—which we too have placed at the center of our analysis—which is supposed to provide the motor force. Wasn't it the accumulation of capital which led from the poverty of the Middle Ages to the affluence of today's advanced capitalist countries? And aren't the multinational corporate giants of our time infinitely more effective accumulators than the relative pygmies that pioneered the economic development of Western Europe, North America, and Japan? And if this is so, aren't we justified in looking forward to rapid progress and a happy ending?

The answer, unfortunately, is no—flatly and unconditionally. Multinational capital in migrating to the Third World today has absolutely no intention or interest in transforming those societies. It plans to adapt to and exploit the conditions which exist there. Whatever transformation takes place is a by-product of this process and cannot but intensify rather than alleviate the tragic conditions which are already deeply rooted in a long history. The general case can be most effectively presented by means of a particular example, the expansion of foreign (predominantly U.S.) capital into Brazil, one of the biggest and potentially richest countries in the Third World. Multinational corporations based in the advanced capitalist countries go to Brazil to supply and profit from markets which already exist and can be expected to grow with the general expansion of global capitalism. Some of these are domestic Brazilian markets, fueled by the spending of perhaps 20 percent of the population in the highest income brackets. Others are international markets for agricultural products, raw materials, and certain kinds of manufactured goods the costs of which can be kept low through the employment of cheap labor. But there is one market, potentially by far the largest, which does not exist and which the multinational corporations have no intention whatever of creating, the market which would burgeon along with a rising real standard of living for the Brazilian masses. The reason for what may at first sight seem a paradox is simple: for capitalists, both Brazilian and foreign, the masses are looked upon as costs, not as customers: the lower their real wages, the higher the profits from selling to the local upper class and the international market. The vicious dynamic at work here has resulted in a drastic decline in the level of real wages in Brazil since the military coup of 1964, amounting by some estimates to as much as 40 percent. A stunning illustration of what Marx called the general law of capitalist accumulation—growing riches on the one hand, deepening poverty on the other. And Brazil, far from being an exception, is a perfect example of what is happening and will undoubtedly continue to happen throughout the underdeveloped periphery of the world capitalist system.

I think you will agree with me that the conclusion to be drawn from this analysis is obvious. For the great mass of people living in the Third World—and that means for well over half of the human race—who are the special victims of this stage of capitalist development, the only possible way forward is to break out of the straitjacket which has been imposed upon them by the raw power of the metropolitan centers and to enter upon their own self-reliant course of development. This means revolution, the most massive and profound revolution in human history. And that is the final term in the logic of "corporations, the state, and imperialism."

8.
Crisis Within the Crisis

In what follows I assume, without attempting to demonstrate, that the global capitalist system entered a period of crisis in the first half of the 1970s; that this period of crisis will be of long duration, with no end now in sight; that its characteristic features are a retarded rate of capital accumulation (implying, both as cause and as effect, a relatively low rate of profit), rising unemployment, and continuing inflation at rates well above those of the previous quarter century. Economic fluctuations of the familiar business-cycle type continue during such a period of stagnation (as they did, for example, during the stagnant 1930s), and additional shocks and disturbances to the system (crises within the crisis) are not only possible but inevitable.

My immediate focus is on this last phenomenon (crises within the crisis), and my remarks center on the United States, partly because I am most familiar with the situation there, and partly because it is the largest and most influential unit in the global system.

The United States is the only one of the advanced capitalist countries which has experienced a vigorous and still continuing recovery from the cyclical downturn of 1974-1975. This upswing, however, has not been based on a high rate of capital accumulation (private investment) as is the normal pattern, but on increases in consumption and government spending. And these increases, in turn, have been made possible by an unprecedentedly rapid growth of private and government debt. To quote a recent special report in *Business Week* (October 16), the leading U.S.

This note was written for a special issue of *Rinascita*, a weekly publication of the Communist Party of Italy. It appeared in the December 1978 issue of *Monthly Review*.

business journal: "Since late 1975 the U.S. has created a new debt economy, a credit explosion so wild and so eccentric that it dwarfs even the borrowing binge of the early 1970s." At the present time consumer debt (including residential mortgages) amounts to more than $1,000 billion (billion = thousand million), an increase of over 50 percent since 1975; and the debt of the federal government has risen almost 50 percent to $825 billion.

This debt explosion is not limited to the United States. Even more dramatic has been the increase in Euromarket debt (including Eurocurrency bank credit and Euromarket bonds) which, according to *Business Week*'s figures, grew from $34.4 billion in 1975 to an estimated $88 billion in 1978, an increase of 156 percent, with developed and underdeveloped (including OPEC) countries both participating heavily in this borrowing spree.

The following comments will help to throw light on the meaning and implications of these developments.

First, it is clear that in the absence of this multi-faceted debt explosion, not only would the U.S. recovery from the recession of 1974-1975 have been much weaker; this would have been equally true of the global system as a whole, and in the case of many countries there might not have been any recovery at all. There are at least two reasons for this: (a) a weaker U.S. recovery would have meant a reduced volume of U.S. imports, hence a lower demand for the commodities produced by supplier countries (EEC, Japan, OPEC, "Fourth World" raw materials); and (b) without Euromarket loans all these countries would have been forced to restrict their imports, with depressing effects on world markets and world production.

Second, no one believes that debt expansion can continue much longer at the rate of the last three years. But any slowdown in *the rate of expansion* of debt is bound to be reflected in a reduction in *the absolute level* of debt-supported demand for goods and services, since the burden of interest charges plus debt repayment continues for a long time to reduce the amount of spendable income at the disposal of borrowers. It is impossible to predict the precise timing of the slowdown in debt expansion, but certain facts indicate the probability that it will come sooner rather than later: these are, first, that the next phase of the business cycle is almost certain to be a downswing; and, second, that at least in the United States there is a growing consensus among observers of the economic scene that the onset of this new phase could come in the very near future. A normal cyclical downturn coinciding with a slowdown in the current rate of debt expansion could trigger a recession at least as sharp as that of 1974-1975.

But this is not all. The world debt structure has been ballooning more or less continuously ever since the long post-Second World War boom began more than a quarter of a century ago: in fact this debt-expansion process has been one of the crucial forces sustaining the boom. But we know from long historical experience that as debt structures expand they develop more and more weak spots and that eventually there comes a time when these weak spots begin to give way, threatening the whole structure with collapse. It is not hard to point to many such weak spots at the present time. In the United States, for example, there is widespread concern that consumers are now so deeply in debt that a serious cyclical recession would bring on a wave of defaults and bankruptcies. And on the international scene the situation of many borrowing countries in the Third and Fourth Worlds is precarious in the extreme. Moreover, once defaults and bankruptcies start on a sufficiently large scale, they can quickly snowball into a full-scale financial panic. This is also a lesson of history which has too often been forgotten in the euphoria of postwar "prosperity." *Business Week* is hardly exaggerating when it says, in the report cited above, that we have now reached a point when, "unless the nation is very lucky indeed, the new debt economy—already more than 50 percent higher than the old [pre-1975] debt economy—could come crashing down." What is said of the nation could equally well be said of the capitalist world.

One final question has to be raised, though as of now it cannot be answered: if the "crisis within the crisis" which now threatens should develop into a financial crackup, analogous to what happened following the downfall of Austria's Creditanstalt in 1931, would the consequence be a splintering of the world market and the world monetary system, with the development of protectionism, trade wars, currency blocs, and new military adventures such as characterized the 1930s? Or would the advanced capitalist countries be pushed toward closer cooperation in efforts to contain and control the crisis and ultimately to lay the international foundations for a new period of accelerated capital accumulation?

Either course would be filled with pitfalls and obstacles, and of course there would be no guarantee of success even in the narrowest capitalist interpretation of the term. And as far as the masses are concerned, those who are already suffering the effects of the long-term crisis of the global capitalist system, they have nothing to gain from any of capitalism's efforts to save itself. Sooner or later they are going to have to find their own salvation, which can only come through withdrawing from what has become a hopelessly self-contradictory system and beginning the arduous task of building a society which puts the needs and interests of the producers of the world's wealth above the needs and interests of those who now appropriate and misuse it.

9.
The U.S. Dollar, Petrodollars, and U.S. Imperialism

During the first week of November the U.S. government announced a package of strong measures designed to check the seemingly endless downward drift in the international value of the dollar. Washington was well aware that these steps might set off a recession, especially since one of the planned actions was to attract foreign capital by boosting the already high interest rates even higher. But the authorities, who were long held back from decisive action by fear of the consequences of a new recession, were finally confronted by an even greater danger—the likely onset of a world-wide financial panic. In reviewing the background of this reversal from past complacency over the long-run downward gyrations of the dollar in the international money markets, the *Wall Street Journal* (November 6, 1978) observed:

> Pessimism about the dollar and the administration's economic management had become so rampant that the nation was on the brink of, in the words of one New York banker, "a nineteenth-century kind of financial panic from which a genuine depression could have developed."

When all is said and done, however, the best that the new program can, or for that matter is intended to, accomplish is a temporary rescue operation. The reason for saying this is that, despite all the bold pronouncements, nothing substantial is being undertaken to tackle the underlying forces that in the first place

This is in the main a reconstruction, with a few additions, from notes of a talk given in Minneapolis on October 28, 1978, at the annual convention of the Association of Arab-American University Graduates. It originally appeared in the January 1979 issue of *Monthly Review*.

have been propelling the dollar on its downward course. The speculators, including the multinational corporations and banks, have been behaving with normal capitalist rationality in response to a fundamental weakness of the dollar. They have been selling dollars in exchange for stronger currencies because they have been anticipating, and meanwhile contributing to, ever greater weakness of the dollar. There are two main proximate reasons for this weakness: first, a huge increase in the deficits in the U.S. balance of payments during the last two years; and second, the related and ever-growing surplus of dollars abroad, which represent a staggering mountain of U.S. liabilities.

It must be understood, however, that both of these reasons are only surface phenomena. At bottom, as will be explained later, the causes are to be found in current and past practices of U.S. imperialism. The U.S. ruling class has of course no intention of breaking with imperialism. In fact, its major aim is to hold on to as much as possible of its insecure hegemonic role in the world capitalist system. That being the case, the decision-makers are unable to cope in any significant way with either the pile-up of dollars abroad or the huge balance-of-payments deficits. Instead, the tendency in Washington, on Wall Street, and among bourgeois economists is to look for scapegoats. These substitute "explanations" for the dollar's troubles serve not only to cover up the root causes, they also help rationalize the shifting of the burdens of imperialism's crises to the Third World and the domestic working class.

The scapegoats emerge mainly from two commonly accepted explanations of current difficulties. First is the claim that U.S. exports are lagging because its industries are becoming less competitive—an argument that rests in large measure on complaints about the laxity of the working class and a supposed resulting drag on productivity. Second is the blame put on the jump in oil prices, which happened to coincide with increasing dependence by the United States on oil imports.

Neither of these cover-ups, however, can stand up against either fact or reason. The talk about the relative loss of competitive ability by U.S. industry completely overlooks the overwhelming role of the multinational corporations in world trade. (The facts on this will be presented later on.) Apart from that, it should be recalled, the dollar's illness set in long before one could by the farthest stretch of the imagination complain about the efficiency of U.S. industry. The practice of living with perpetual balance-of-payments deficits, and therefore also with the piling-up of dollars abroad, began in the early 1950s. The official policy toward the potential danger of such behavior was typical of a hegemonic imperialist power: nothing serious would ensue because the rest of the world, including allies, could either like it or lump it.

But this attitude did not make the problem disappear. Disturbances in the international money markets began to crop up more and more frequently in the late 1960s. The crisis signals accelerated as the United States expanded its overseas expenditures for the seemingly endless invasion of Vietnam. By mid-1971 a critical boiling point was reached, resulting in the break-up of the post-Second World War international money system and the initiation of the first of two formal dollar devaluations. Neither of these rescue operations, however, served to get rid of the chronic balance-of-payments deficits and the dollar's weakness. All of this, remember, occurred well before the hike in oil prices at the end of 1973.

Against this background, the most that might reasonably be argued is that the increasing burden of larger and higher-priced oil imports worsened a long-standing bad situation. But there are still more telling reasons for rejecting the misconceptions about the presumed responsiblity of higher oil prices. For example, consider the following: only 23 percent of the total energy requirements of the United States are met by oil imports, whereas this percentage is 92 percent for Japan and 67 percent for West Germany. (*The Economist,* July 8, 1978) If oil prices and heavy dependency on oil imports were the decisive influences on the international value of a country's currency, then one should expect the Japanese yen and the German mark, instead of the U.S. dollar, to have come tumbling down. What happened, obviously, was just the opposite.

But one need not rely on such indirect reasoning to expose the fallacy about the huge expenditure for oil imports being the cause of the more recent U.S. balance-of-payments deficits and of the dollar's downfall. For, as we shall see, the simple fact is that the oil-exporting nations have been returning more dollars to the United States than they have been receiving for their oil shipments to this country.

By now it should be clear that we have to dig deeper to understand the frailty, as well as the remaining strength, of the dollar. Above all, we need to grasp and keep in mind a basic aspect of international money matters, one that is too often obscured by the maze of technical details that complicate such discussions. Fortunately, every once in a while the rockbottom truth shines through the technical intricacies, and this is more likely to happen at critical turning points. Thus, for example, when the IMF became embroiled in debate among the leading imperialist powers on how to cope with the mounting difficulties occasioned by U.S. arrogance in international monetary affairs, a senior economist at the Standard Oil Company (New Jersey)—now Exxon Corporation—pointed out:

> We may ask why, after a hundred years of international monetary conferences, men still have not resolved their differences. The answer lies in one word—*power*. That is what one hundred years of international monetary conferences have been about. The 22nd annual meeting of the International Monetary Fund held at Rio, where a new facility for creating international liquidity was recommended, is no exception to this general rule.*

A similar rule holds not just for the occasional conference but for the whole history of international money relations, because a country's dominance in this area is an enormously important source of additional power and wealth. Let us turn to a simple

---

*Eugene A. Birnbaum, "Gold and the International Monetary System: An Orderly Reform" (International Finance Section, Princeton University: *Essays in International Finance,* No. 66, April 1968), p. 2. After making the above statement, the author proceeds to claim that there is one exception to the rule that the struggle for power is what it is all about: the United Nations Monetary and Financial Conference at Bretton Woods! This is a surprising opinion (perhaps not so surprising, coming as it does from a North American) about the conference that established the institutional framework for the long-lasting U.S. financial hegemony after the Second World War.

illustration to explain this. Suppose an individual has no savings, yet indulges in spending $15,000 a year while earning only $10,000. Clearly, this can be done only by someone who has access to credit. And unless he or she has a rich and magnanimous relative, such overspending cannot continue for too many years. Before long, the source of credit is bound to dry up and the accumulated debt must be repaid, with interest. If this individual's earnings do not increase, then the accumulated debt can only be paid off by a reduction in current spending below $10,000 a year—in other words, by belt-tightening.

This type of constraint to spending applies equally to most nations. In the normal course of events, a country can buy in international markets only an amount equal in value to what it can sell in those markets. In the absence of sufficient reserves from past savings, overbuying results in debt and, all other things being equal, in a reduction in living standards when the debt has to be repaid.

There are, however, exceptional nations that are able to live to a considerable extent outside the limits of this elementary "law" of economics. These are the countries whose *domestic paper currency* also functions as *international money.* In the economics trade, money that functions in this way is called a "key currency." Notably since the middle of the nineteenth century, the domestic money of some of the more powerful nations has served as key currencies. That is, throughout the capitalist world these currencies were accepted in addition to, and as a substitute for, gold and silver: (1) as a means of settling international transactions (e.g., in payment for imports and debt service), and (2) as a reserve to cope with trade-balance fluctuations.*

It should be obvious that a key-currency country obtains clear-cut advantages. It can operate in the arena of international commerce and finance with a much greater degree of freedom than a run-of-the-mill nation, let alone a Third World country. If it overbuys from other countries, it can pay for these purchases by

---

*For information on the extensive use of key currencies even in the heyday of the gold standard, see Peter H. Lindert, "Key Currencies and Gold, 1900–1913" (International Finance Section, Princeton University: *Princeton Studies in International Finance,* No. 24, August 1969).

merely printing or otherwise creating more domestic money. It therefore can live for long periods quite comfortably with balance-of-payments deficits; instead of having to tighten its belt, it can become wealthier from an excess of imports over exports. Even more important, the ability to create unilaterally additional international money expands a country's ability to export capital, thereby enabling it to obtain assets yielding a steady return flow of interest and dividends.

Such power, to be sure, does not come out of the blue: not every country can elect to be a key-currency country. It arises from, and in turn helps maintain and enhance, a dominant world position in industrial production, in international trade and transportation, in empire, and in military power. At the same time, this type of dominance is never absolute and secure. Wars, the crises endemic to capitalism, and the continuing pressure of rivals—all these create the prerequisites for a shake-up in the hierarchical relations among the core counties of the imperialist system. The benefits attached to a top position in the hierarchy and the opportunities that arise from the changing fortunes of the capitalist nations set the stage for recurrent power struggles, and notably the struggle which arises from the determination of the top dog in the international money system to hold on to its privileges against the biting and snapping of hungry rivals.

In essence, what is happening in today's financial markets reflects a struggle of this last type. The top-dog position of the United States was unchallenged during the first two decades after the Second World War. The U.S. bid for leadership had already emerged early in the century, and the years between the two world wars were marked by increasing rivalry between New York and London for financial ascendancy. Building on the disorder of the Great Depression and the destruction of the Second World War, the United States reached by mid-century unparalleled supremacy in production, trade, military, and financial affairs. And the power that came with this supremacy was exercised without inhibitions and with unprecedented arrogance.

On the financial front this meant carrying on with an uninterrupted balance-of-payments deficit beginning in the early 1950s, and covering these deficits by flooding the banks of the rest of the capitalist world with U.S. dollars. The disturbances in world finance of recent years (and of today) are the inevitable consequences of this history, along with growing reluctance of rival powers to continue playing the game of follow the leader.

It is true that, looked at from an imperialist point of view, the United States has had unusually heavy international obligations. In the old days of colonialism, the mother country financed the costs of occupation and of additional colony-grabbing by taxing the natives. Furthermore, owning a colony automatically provided the metropole's capitalists with privileged market, finance, and investment preserves. Decolonization changed all that. Even though it opened up potentially vast new opportunities for U.S. business as against rivals from the old colonial powers, the exercise of control and influence in the Third World now called for large-scale spending for military and economic "aid." Also, along with the disruption of the Second World War and the spread of the national liberation movements came the real and, even more, the potential narrowing down of space for capitalist enterprise. Much money was therefore needed to operate military bases around the globe to contain the spread of socialism. Finally, the era of the multinational corporation had dawned, and giant U.S. corporations sought the wherewithal to move freely in foreign lands.

All of this heavy spending abroad became feasible for the United States as soon as the dollar blossomed after the Second World War into *the,* not just *a,* key currency of international finance. As a result, the United States could live year in and year out with balance-of-payments deficts. All that was needed was to create more dollars (either through the Federal Reserve Board or the expansion of domestic bank credit), which when shipped abroad had to be accepted, under the Bretton Woods system, by foreign banks as if they were as good as gold. The upshot of this method of financing U.S. imperialism, plus the foreign operations of U.S. multinational corporations and banks, is that by now the amount of dollars floating around Europe is almost as large as, if not larger than, the narrowly defined money supply within the United States itself. In the United States there are today about $360 billion in currency and checking accounts. In European banks, on the other hand, there were at the end of 1977, according to the very conservative estimates of the Bank for International Settlements, at least $270 billion of U.S. money (called Eurodollars). Others (e.g., the *Wall Street Journal,* November 20, 1978) estimate that there are now over $500 billion on deposit outside the United States.

What needs to be understood is that it is precisely this fantastic and continuing accumulation of dollars abroad that underlies the instability of the dollar in foreign markets. For example, today about 80 percent of the reserves held by central banks around the capitalist world are in the form of U.S. dollars. Given the volume and endless growth of U.S. dollars abroad, central bankers are impelled by the simplest rules of financial prudence to diversify their holdings. In fact, the diversification process has already begun: only a few years ago as much as 90 percent of their reserves were in U.S. dollars. But this very process of diversification helps push the international value of the dollar down, and this drop in dollar value erodes the worth of the remaining dollars held by foreigners.

The capitalist world's central bankers are therefore on the horns of a dilemma. Too fast or too large a sale of the dollars they hold could disrupt foreign-exchange markets, lead to panic and crisis, and undermine the reserves they count on for their own stability. On the other hand, they are choked up with dollar reserves and they sit in fear that they will be caught with their pants down when other dollar holders or speculators sell off dollars. To a greater or lesser degree, the same dilemma faces all other big dollar holders overseas, who are caught between fear of further decline of the dollar and concern about protecting their dollar assets.

In sum, these are the contradictory forces that are at the heart of the dollar problem. For it is as a result of past and present practices of U.S. imperialism that (1) the dollar sinks in value as foreign holders seek to protect themselves against the inevitable impact of the unending dollar accumulation, and (2) the dollar nevertheless, and precisely because of the vast size of these dollar holdings, remains the key currency of international finance. Considering the overwhelming importance of these dollar-crises-producing phenomena, it is indeed ironic for the onus of

Table 9-1
Financial Transactions Between the
United States and OPEC Countries
(1974 to 1977 Combined)

Money Moving from the United States	*Money Returning to the United States*
U.S. Purchases of Goods and Services .... $106 billion	Purchases of Goods and Services by OPEC Countries .... $ 70 billion
	Investments in the United States by OPEC Countries .... $ 38 billion
Total .... $106 billion	Total .... $108 billion

Source: Christopher L. Bach, "OPEC Transactions in the U.S. International Accounts, 1972–77," *Survey of Current Business,* April 1978, pp. 21–32.

the problem to be placed on such factors as oil imports and labor productivity.

As for the question of the impact of oil imports, the facts are simple and clear. They can be seen in Table 9–1, which summarizes the transactions between the United States and the members of OPEC (Organization of Petroleum Exporting Countries) from 1974 to 1977. Since the leap in oil prices started towards the end of 1973, its full effect was first felt in 1974. We end with 1977 because all the necessary data are not yet in for 1978. The story for just the four years covered, however, is a convincing enough refutation of what has become a popular fallacy.

As can be seen from the left-hand section of Table 9–1, the United States spent $106 billion in OPEC countries from 1974 to 1977. Almost all of this was for the import of oil. There were some relatively minor purchases of services, primarily about $1 billion to pay for labor and materials in Saudi Arabia in connection with the installation of U.S. armaments.

The return flow of money from the OPEC countries is shown in the right-hand section of Table 9–1. There we see that during the same period the OPEC countries sent back $70 billion to the United States for goods and services. Almost three fifths (58 percent) of this was spent for merchandise such as capital goods, autos, consumer goods, and armaments from private manufacturers. These purchases were made primarily by Saudi Arabia, Venezuela, and Iran. A little over 27 percent of the return flow went to U.S. firms for dividends, interest, fees, and royalties. Another 13 percent was used to purchase armaments under U.S. government military-agency sales contracts, principally to Iran and Saudi Arabia. The remainder of the $70 billion was for miscellaneous services.

The net result of these back and forth sales was a U.S. deficit of $36 billion ($106 billion minus $70 billion). But this deficit was more than wiped out by the $38 billion of OPEC countries' investments in the United States. This was money placed in U.S. banks or used to purchase U.S. treasury bonds and corporate securities. Department of Commerce statisticians have been unable to obtain reliable estimates of other investments such as real estate in the United States by the oil exporters. But even disregarding this additional return flow of dollars, it should be evident enough that the large increase in U.S. spending for oil between 1974 and 1977 was definitely *not* the cause of the overall balance-of-payments deficits.

It is probable that OPEC member countries, like central bankers and multinational firms, began to shift out of dollars towards the end of 1977. But this was clearly a defensive move in reaction to the decline in the international value of the dollar that had begun much earlier in the year. The overriding fact is that the OPEC countries are necessarily integrated in the dollar system. For example, some 60 percent of the $160 billion of foreign assets held by OPEC countries is in dollar accounts, either in the United States or in Europe. (*Euromoney*, May 1978, p. 36) Equally significant is the flat statement made by Sheik Ali Khalifa Al-Sabah, president of OPEC's Committee of Experts: "There is no probability of abandoning the dollar as a means of payment. It is the only currency in which such huge transactions can take place." (*Business Week*, July 24, 1978, p. 138)

The other scapegoat—the alleged declining competitiveness of U.S. industry— also falls to the ground when exposed to a few basic facts. This argument clearly concerns exports of manufactures, since it would have little meaning if applied to exports of agricultural products or materials. Before we get to the substance of our case, it would be useful to point out that over half of U.S. manufacturing exports generally consist of capital goods. It should come as no surprise that exports of such goods have been sluggish in recent years. The reason for this has nothing to do with the alleged lack of competitiveness of U.S. industry and everything to do with the existence of industrial overcapacity in all the advanced capitalist countries. The onset of stagnation and the sluggish recovery from the recent recession have dampened the demand for capital goods, and this naturally shows up as lagging exports of U.S. capital goods.*

But an even more important aspect of this question has been almost completely ignored. And that is the large extent to which U.S. manufacturers are not competing for export business against foreign firms but against their own branches and affiliates located abroad. Just look at the facts shown in Table 9–2: *U.S. manufacturing firms located abroad are selling almost three times as much as is being exported from the United States.* Note also that this ratio has moved up from 1.9 in 1960 to 2.8 in 1976, the last date for which statistics are currently available.

What has been happening, quite clearly, is that U.S capital has been shifting from export activity to capturing markets abroad, or taking advantage of cheaper labor, by establishing factories in foreign lands. This is not because of any lack of competitiveness of U.S. industry, but because of the profit-making strategy of giant oligopolistic corporations. As part of this strategy, U.S. multinationals have indeed been exporting—from their overseas subsidiaries. Look, for example, how the $212.8 billion sales by U.S. foreign affiliates in 1976 were distributed: $161 billion worth of manufactured goods were sold in the countries in which the

---

*This is also the judgment of the Bank for International Settlements. According to its annual report (June 12, 1978),p. 68: "U.S. export sales have been held back by the low level of fixed investment in the rest of the industrialized world."

Table 9-2

Exports vs. Sales by Firms Located Abroad: Manufactures

	(1) U.S. Exports	*(2)* Sales by Foreign Affiliates of U.S. Firms	*(3)* Ratio of Foreign Sales to Exports *(2) ÷ (1)*
	— in billions of dollars —		
1960	12.3	23.6	1.9
1965	17.2	42.4	2.5
1970	29.1	78.3	2.7
1976	76.6	212.8	2.8

Source: Export data from *International Economic Report of the President* (January 1977). Sales by foreign affiliates from *Survey of Business,* September 1962, November 1966, and March 1978.

affiliates were located; $14.1 billion exported to the United States; and $37.7 billion exported to other countries. (*Survey of Current Business,* March 1978)

Looked at purely as a game of numbers, the U.S. balance-of-payments deficits would soon disappear if the $37.7 billion of the export activity of the multinationals abroad, let alone a portion of the $161 billion they sell in the countries where they are located, were replaced by exports from the United States. But of course capitalist firms, and especially monopolistic corporations, do not work that way.

We cannot in the present context explore further all the complexities of the U.S. balance-of-payments problem. But the foregoing example of the manufacturing export situation puts the case in a nutshell. The way growth of multinationals has been financed is but one of many imperialist practices that have contributed to the problems of the dollar. The ruling class of an advanced capitalist society such as the United States cannot, nor does it want to, overcome its imperialist nature. The fundamental ills of the international money system therefore cannot be cured; the most that can be done is some tinkering in the hope of averting a major crisis. Meanwhile, confronted with the contradictions of its behavior as a hegemonic power, the U.S. ruling class seeks to divert attention from root causes to false issues from which some side benefits might be obtained. In particular, the hue and cry about the alleged declining competitiveness of domestic industry can serve to pave the way for increased exploitation of the working class and for tax relief for business ostensibly needed to modernize industry.

10.
On the New Global Disorder

"A few years ago," wrote financial reporter Ann Crittenden in the *New York Times* of February 4, 1979, "an agressive group of less developed countries began demanding a new economic order. What they wanted was some formal restructuring to give poorer nations a bigger slice of the pie. This implied that world leaders had some rational control over events. It is now apparent that the old order is indeed crumbling—but amid such disorientation that the world is confronted not with a new order but a new global disorder."

If we are to think clearly about the changing world we live in, I believe the first requirement is that we seek to understand the causes and nature of this new global disorder. In what follows I shall focus on what is surely the most important source of the phenomenon, i.e., the multiple crises of the capitalist system.

Here we must never lose from sight that capitalism is not a national system, nor is it a collection of discrete capitalist countries, some underdeveloped, some developing. It is a *system* in which all these are linked together. This system has an overall structure, its parts are interrelated in definite ways, and it has what Marx called "laws of motion."

The overall structure can best be understood in terms of the center-periphery metaphor. The transition from the center to the periphery is not clear-cut or abrupt but rather takes the form

This is a slightly revised version of a statement prepared for the twentieth anniversary commemorative issue of the *Asahi Journal,* published by the Tokyo newspaper, *Asahi Shimbun.* The statement is a condensation of a lecture delivered at a number of universities during February 1979. It appeared in the April 1979 issue of *Monthly Review.*

of concentric rings which merge into each other. At the center of the center is the hegemonic power—in the present historical phase the United States of America—with the greatest concentration of wealth and military power. Around it are grouped the secondary imperialist powers—Germany, Japan, Britain, France, Holland. Next come the less powerful developed capitalist countries—the Scandinavian countries, Belgium, Switzerland, Austria, Italy, Greece, Spain, Portugal, Canada, Australia. Beyond this is where the periphery begins. The inner ring of the periphery consists of what may be called regional subimperialist countries— Mexico, Brazil, Israel, Saudi Arabia, Iran (until recently), perhaps India.* And finally there are outer rings of the periphery comprising the great majority of underdeveloped Third World countries in Asia, Africa, and Latin America. All of these taken together make up a coherent whole, with lines of authority and subordination running from the center of the center clear out to the edges of the periphery. Generally speaking there is a reverse flow of money and its counterpart, real wealth, from the outer edges of the periphery through the intermediate rings to the center and finally the center of the center. The whole constitutes on the one hand a pyramid of power and wealth and on the other hand a system of exploitation of weaker by stronger at every stage of the transition from center to periphery and from bottom to top.

The global capitalist system is not only structured, it is also highly dynamic. The motor force driving it forward is *accumulation of capital*. Every unit of capital, wherever located, has an inherent urge to expand. Not all succeed. Some fall by the wayside or are swallowed up by more efficient or more ruthless rivals. But all try, and the ones that survive are the successful ones. By the same token, every capitalist country, made up as it is of units of capital, must always be tending to expand. But not all at the same rate. So there is unevenness in rates of growth, hence also in the distribution of wealth and power. And the countries which

---

*The classification of South Africa presents difficulties: it is *both* a "less powerful developed capitalist country" *and* a "regional subimperialist country." In some ways it can even be looked upon as an empire in and of itself—an advanced capitalist white economy holding onto and seeking to expand its own periphery in the black states of southern Africa.

are relatively more dynamic are the ones that seek to improve their standing at the expense of others. This is why there can never be a settling down of the system as a whole, never an equilibrium that is more than temporary and precarious.

The capital-accumulation process does not proceed smoothly *within* capitalist countries any more than it does *between* them. It is fraught with what Marxists call "contradictions," which cause it to run in the form of short cycles and long waves, and which from time to time generate more serious blockages and crises.

The force which dominates and shapes the development of the system as a whole is the capital-accumulation process in the advanced countries of the center. For the most part the periphery reacts and adapts to what happens in the center. Or, in other words, the center enjoys a large degree of independence, while the periphery has little or no independence. It follows that for the countries and peoples of the periphery, independence can be gained—if it can be achieved at all—only by breaking out of the system and starting on a fresh foundation. It further follows that to the extent the peoples of the periphery aspire to independence—and the drive in that direction seems to be strong and persistent—they can realistically pursue their objective only by actively revolting against the economic and political ties which bind them to the global capitalist system.

Let me now review very briefly the historical development of the global capitalist system. The formative period begins in the late fifteenth and early sixteenth centuries with the overseas expansion of the European mercantilist states—Spain, Portugal, Holland, France, Britain. Colonial empires were built, and the nascent capitalist countries of what would become today's center fought it out for hegemony. Finally, following France's defeat in the Napoleonic wars, Britain emerged as the clearly dominant power. This situation lasted until roughly the last quarter of the nineteenth century when a fresh burst of external expansion and colonization erupted, accompanied by a renewed struggle for hegemony—this time among Britain, France, Germany, and the United States, with Japan soon joining the fray as the first non-white imperialist power of modern times.

This phase culminated in the First World War which marked

the defeat of Germany's bid for hegemony, the rise of the United States to rough parity with Britain, the far-reaching reshuffling of colonies and spheres of influence in the periphery, and (significant augury of things to come) the Russian Revolution and the first massive breakaway from the global system itself.

For a few years during the 1920s a relative equilibrium was established under what was in effect a shared Anglo-American hegemony.* But it was extraordinarily short-lived. The rise of Nazism in Germany signaled a second German bid for supremacy, this time in alliance with Japan, whose ambitions to profit from the outcome of the First World War in the Far East had been thwarted by superior Anglo-American naval power, and which had launched its campaign to subjugate China in 1931. This renewed struggle for hegemony led directly to the Second World War.

It was the Second World War which set the stage for the development of the situation which is the focus of our present attention. Let me list in shorthand form what I see as the decisive results of that world-wide conflict: (1) defeat of the Berlin-Tokyo axis; (2) weakening of Britain and France; (3) rise of the United States to undisputed hegemony; (4) defection of China from the global capitalist system; (5) maturing in the periphery of national liberation struggles (some with origins as far back as the turn of the century) resulting in a continuing process of replacement of colonialism by neocolonialism.

The period of undisputed U.S. hegemony lasted somewhat more than a quarter of a century, after which it began to weaken as the defeated powers of the Second World War gradually recovered their strength. The global capitalist system always works most smoothly when there is one undisputed hegemonic power, and the eroding and ending of that undisputed hegemony always signals the onset of a time of troubles and crises. The post-Second World War period has been no exception.

Under U.S. hegemony global capitalism had the benefits of a

---

*Hegemony was shared vis-à-vis other advanced capitalist countries (e.g., the naval treaty of 1922 prescribing Anglo-American naval superiority over Japan) and also vis-à-vis peripheral areas, but this did not eliminate intense rivalry between the United States and Britain in such fields as the discovery and control of the world's petroleum resources.

functioning and flexible international monetary system and a relatively free flow of international trade and capital movements. Gold and the dollar were established by the Bretton Woods agreements as interchangeable forms of universal money. The growth of trade and payments created a great demand for an increased supply of universally acceptable forms of money. The United States could and did satisfy this demand by running deficits in its balance of payments, thus pushing dollars out into the economies and banking systems of the rest of the world. For the United States this privilege was a source of enormous power, enabling the country to draw on the resources of the world almost at will. It was also a source of temptation and danger. The temptation was to abuse the privilege; the danger was that abuse would wreck the system. As we shall see, the temptation was too great for the United States to resist.

But a workable monetary system and relatively free trade were not the only conditions favoring the accumulation of capital in the post-Second World War period. There were also the following to be considered:

First, the need to repair the damage inflicted by the fighting and to make up for civilian shortages caused by diversion of resources to military production during the war.

Second, the availability of a great array of new capital-using technologies emerging from wartime developments (electronics, jet planes, etc.).

Third, the enormous demands created by the military needs of the hegemonic power (and to a lesser extent its military allies). These needs are inherent in the hegemonic position itself and have been greatly swelled by the special conditions of this period, especially (a) the emergence of the Soviet Union as a noncapitalist military/economic superpower, and (b) the spread of national liberation struggles and the efforts of the imperialist powers to defeat these struggles, involving two major regional wars (Korea and Vietnam) and many smaller military confrontations.

Against this background we can understand how it came to pass that the end of the Second World War opened a period of unprecedented expansion and prosperity for the global capitalist system. Ever since 1945 the upswings of the business cycle have been long by historical standards, the downswings short and shallow. The contradictions of capitalism seemed to have been so much reduced, if not actually eliminated, that they could realistically be thought of as a thing of the past.

But underneath, and mostly out of sight, certain long-term tendencies were at work which pointed to stormy weather ahead. I shall treat these under the following headings: (1) overinvestment, (2) pile-up of debts, (3) weakening of the international monetary system, (4) growing inequality between center and periphery.

Overinvestment. In the heady atmosphere of those years, optimism pervaded the business world in all parts of the global system. Capitalists built for a supposedly endlessly expanding economy. Enormous amounts of capital equipment were constructed, especially in basic industries like steel, shipbuilding, motor cars, heavy chemicals, etc. Such an investment boom creates exaggerated prosperity in the short and medium runs, adding fuel to its own fire (expanding the steel industry requires much steel, etc.). But as innumerable historical experiences have shown, it cannot go on forever; and when it becomes clear that enough is enough, the letdown is likely to be all the more jolting.

Pile-up of Debt. This took place both on a national and on an international scale. To quote from a special report in the prestigious U.S. journal *Business Week* (October 16, 1978): "Since late 1975 the United States has created a new debt economy, a credit explosion so wild and so eccentric that it dwarfs even the borrowing binge of the early 1970s." And internationally, a "massive flow of funds from the international market . . . is enabling nations to keep rolling over old debt and taking on new debt nearly without limit. In just four years, the industrialized countries of the world have doubled their Euromarket debt, the less developed countries . . . that do not export oil have tripled their Euromarket debt, and now even many of the OPEC nations themselves are borrowing on so vast a scale that they will owe nearly $10 billion by the end of this year [1978], compared to a mere $900 million in 1974." All this borrowing of course has sustained international demand and investment, but no one can imagine that it can go on without limit.

Weakening of the International Monetary System. For many reasons, some touched upon above, the United States has continued to run huge balance-of-payments deficits and hence to flood the world with dollars far beyond the needs of the international monetary system. By now estimates of the total amount of dollars floating around the world outside the United States run as high as $600–$700 billion, sums far beyond the power of the United States to control, still less to liquidate. They are and will remain a sword of Damocles hanging over the head of the dollar. At almost any time the near-panic selling of dollars of last October can resume, and at some point there is the ever-present possibility of a full-scale monetary panic, with what consequences we can imagine by going back to what happened after the last comparable incident, i.e., the collapse of the Austrian Creditanstalt in 1931, which triggered the end of the monetary system of the post-First World War period and initiated the new period of protectionism, currency blocs, and national controls over the flows of money and capital.

Growing Inequality between Center and Periphery. The much commented-on widening of the gap between developed and underdeveloped countries has exacerbated the tensions and contradictions of the system as a whole, and has given a powerful impetus to national liberation struggles aimed at escaping from the times and constraints of the global capitalist network. The reason for this growing gap has not been that the periphery was excluded from the accumulation process of those years. But in the underdeveloped countries this took its own special forms, mostly under the aegis of multinational corporations based in the center and aiming not to develop the periphery but to increase their own profits. In pursuit of this purpose the multinational corporations invest in the periphery to serve two kinds of markets: (1) the consumption requirements of small indigenous upper-income groups which have traditionally imported their luxury goods (automobiles, appliances, etc.), and (2) international markets in which demand comes from outside. The great mass of people—workers, peasants, unemployed—do not provide attractive markets for the multinationals: in fact, they count mainly as costs of production so that the multinationals attempt in whatever way they can to keep their wages and the prices of their products as low as possible. Capitalist industrialization in the Third World therefore typically goes hand in hand with the ruthless exploitation of indigenous human and natural resources. The appropriate, indeed necessary, complement of this kind of economic development is the brutal police-military dictatorship which is fast becoming the norm throughout the capitalist-dominated regions of Asia, Africa, and Latin America.

The upshot of all these coexisting, and largely interacting, trends and tendencies is twofold. *In the center*—faltering accumulation, stagflation, and an out-of-control explosion of the debt structure.* *In the periphery*—declining real standards of living for the masses; astronomical rates of unemployment, often reaching 30 to 40 percent of the labor force; misery, malnutrition, and even starvation, with no let-up in sight or improvement in prospect. Both parts of the system are in full crisis, each in its own way, and hence so is the system as a whole.

That breaking points are already being reached is shown by the near U.S. stock-market and dollar panics of the last week in October on the one hand, and by the violent turmoil in Iran since November on the other. The former was checked, at least temporarily, by unusually vigorous action by the American government, but there is unfortunately no reason to expect or even hope that the measures taken have changed or could change the underlying situation. The latter, Iran, reached the point of full-scale revolution by the beginning of 1979.

But apart from the specifics of the present situation and what may happen in the near future, there is a much larger question at issue. The present crisis of the global capitalist system is the result of forces which have been at work for more than a quarter of a century. They are still at work, in fact they are inherent in the system itself. Unless something totally unexpected, like a major war, intervenes, they will continue to work. They cannot be stopped or controlled by national governments, and there is no such thing as an international government.

---

*Stagnation and inflation (stagflation) and the rise of debt are all interrelated functionally as well as temporally in the economies of advanced capitalism. The system's response to lagging demand and rising unemployment is to stimulate public and private buying through expansionary fiscal and monetary policies which involve burgeoning debts. Oligopolistic market structures translate these pressures into price inflation which soon develops a self-propelling character which resists all efforts at control short of a full-scale crisis and collapse.

11.
Productivity Slowdown: A False Alarm

The recovery from the severe recession of 1974–1975 has been unable to solve two of the most persistent and oppressive diseases of the U.S. (and the world capitalist) economy. Employment did pick up as production advanced, but not enough to eliminate mass unemployment. And inflation keeps on going from bad to worse. What's wrong? Why can't something be done about these evils? A large part of the answer, according to our eminent thinkers and influential policy-makers, lies in a supposed slowing down of labor productivity: workers are simply not producing enough. Thus the *New York Times'* lead story on January 26, 1979, introduced its description of the President's Annual Economic Report to Congress with the following opening sentence: "The Carter Administration told Congress today that lagging economic productivity had reduced the country's capacity to create more jobs and higher living standards." In fact, Carter went further, tying the issue of productivity to inflation:

> If we ignore the realities of slower productivity growth—if governments continue to press forward with unabated claims on resources and private citizens continue to demand large gains in money incomes—our inflationary problem will worsen.

Such pronouncements come not only from the White House. They have also been pouring out of diverse "authoritative" sources at an increasing rate in the last few years. Back in 1977, a *Business Week* (February 19, 1977) editorial put it simply and directly:

This article originally appeared in the June 1979 issue of *Monthly Review*.

As a matter of simple arithmetic, there is only one way the United States can achieve its goal of rising incomes with stable prices: It must increase the output per man-hour of its workers—that is to say, raise productivity.

And as this is being written, a major round-up article in the Business Section of the *New York Times* (May 8, 1979) informs us that "experts warn nation about slower growth":

Economists, businessmen, and government officials have become concerned about a marked drop in the nation's productivity growth rate, a development they fear will reduce economic growth and increase inflation and unemployment.

Before we begin to analyze the validity of what has thus become an accepted tenet of the conventional wisdom, it should be noted that what is being discussed is not a *decline* in labor productivity. Even if we accept the official statistics at face value, all that is being claimed is that the rate of *increase* in labor productivity in recent years has not been as large as it was in the early postwar decades. It is this slowdown in the rate of growth of output per man-hour that is claimed to be at the root of the economy's recent troubles. If we look more closely, however, we find that this "fact" is a phoney based upon statistical mystification and involving woefully fallacious thinking.

Productivity and Inflation

Let us first of all get rid of the notion that the presumed slowdown in productivity has anything whatever to do with the persistence and more recently the acceleration of inflation. There are three main ways in which productivity and prices are or might be related to each other. First, there is the effect on prices of wages growing at a faster rate than productivity. In this case, assuming unwillingness on the part of capitalists to see their profits reduced, prices would rise. A second influence of productivity on prices could arise in a situation in which production is insufficient to meet demand. On this assumption, an increase in productivity might be translated into an increase in supply, which in turn would hold down price rises. The third way would involve

Table 11-1
Productivity vs. Real Earnings of Nonagricultural Workers
in Private Industry

Year	Productivity Index (Output per man-hour) 1967 = 100	Gross Average Weekly Earnings[a] 1967 Dollars	Index 1967 = 100
1967	100.0	$101.84	100.0
1970	103.1	103.04	101.2
1975	110.5	101.45	99.6
1978	116.5	104.30	102.4

(a) These are weekly earnings before payroll deductions for social security taxes and for federal, state, and local income taxes.
Source: The productivity index is from the *Economic Report of the President, January 1979* (Washington, D.C.: U.S. Government Printing Office, 1979). The weekly earnings are from *Monthly Labor Review,* March 1979.

reduction of prices by capitalists to reflect lower labor costs per unit of output resulting from an increase in productivity.

As to the first point, the facts are quite clear: *real* wages have been lagging behind the growth in productivity. Workers' paychecks have of course been rising, but these increases have been desperately chasing after the upward spiral of prices, barely managing to keep pace with the rising cost of living. Table 11-1 presents real average weekly earnings of nonfarm workers in private industry for selected years in the period 1967–1978. As can be seen, gross average weekly earnings (before payroll deductions) were $101.84 in 1967. Adjusting for the rise in consumer prices, average weekly earnings since then have been merely hovering around the 1967 level; the advance by 1978 was only a little over 2 percent above the 1967 level. Thus the increase in real wages that did take place was obviously insignificant compared with the over-16-percent growth in productivity shown in Table 11-1 for the period 1967–1978.*

---

*Unit labor costs have of course been rising along with the advance of nominal wages (unadjusted for price changes). But the claim that wage increases and a relatively slow growth in labor productivity have damaged the competitive position of U.S. industry is simply not true. The fact is that the rise in productivity has

The second possible relation between productivity and higher prices noted above certainly has no relevance in today's world. Can anyone seriously believe that our inflation is due to shortages of supply? Least of all could this be thought to be the case in 1975, the year of the most severe postwar recession, with an official unemployment rate of 8.5 percent and manufacturing capacity being used at only 73.6 percent of total. And yet that was the year when consumer prices rose by 9.1 percent compared to 5.8 percent the year before—an increase in the rate of inflation of nearly 50 percent. Nor could one rationally argue that an insufficient supply of goods and services caused inflation to flourish during the subsequent recovery period. In 1978, three years after the bottom of the recession, manufacturing firms were operating at only 84 percent of capacity, according to the Federal Reserve Board. With that much idle capacity and with millions of unemployed actively seeking work, there surely is no need to rely on a speed-up in productivity to get more goods and services produced. The real problem confronting business is not how to increase production but how to sell what is already being produced. That is why so much effort has been and continues to be devoted to sales promotion and to the ballooning of consumer credit.*

The third possible connection between productivity and prices has to do with the hypothesis that savings in labor costs arising from greater output per man-hour will end up in price reductions. This was not only reasonable but demonstrably correct—

been combined with an increase in wages *slower* than that in other advanced capitalist countries. The result has been an increase in unit labor costs in the United States *lower* than that in major competing countries. A recent Labor Department study concludes: "With exchange rate changes taken into account, the United States showed the lowest average rate of gain in unit labor costs during 1970–1977, 6 percent per year; Japan had the highest average rate of gain, 17 percent; and the ten foreign countries combined had an average gain of 13 percent." Keith Daly and Arthur Neef, "Productivity and Unit Labor Costs in 11 Industrial Countries," *Monthly Labor Review*, November 1978, p. 17. The ten foreign countries referred to are Canada, Japan, Belgium, Denmark, France, Germany, Italy, Netherlands, Sweden, and the United Kingdom.

*Although economists stress the role of supply shortages as a cause of inflation, things often work the other way around in the world of monopoly capitalism— prices are raised because of *softness* in demand! A few years ago, the leaders of the aluminum industry gave precisely that reason for a new price hike. The latter was needed, they explained, to compensate for a decline in the volume of shipments.

100 years ago. During the quarter century 1873–1898, a period of rapid mechanization of American industry and hence sharply rising labor productivity, wholesale prices declined by nearly 50 percent.* But that was also a period of fierce competition in industry, so fierce indeed that it had already begun to produce its own negation in the form of the great merger movement which transformed U.S. capitalism from its competitive to its monopoly stage. Since the end of the nineteenth century, productivity has continued to increase, but price behavior has been very different. Taking 1898=100, wholesale prices rose to 208 in 1923, 331 in 1948, and 530 in 1973.† There are of course still some old industries in which savings resulting from productivity increases end up in reduced prices. In addition, new industries still go through a competitive phase during which declining labor costs are matched by declining prices. Nowadays, however, the preponderant behavior of business firms is to grab every opportunity to raise prices, whether productivity is going up or down. New models and new packaging are designed not only to defend or increase market shares but also to provide opportunities to hike prices. When Japanese cars become more expensive in the United States because of the decline of the dollar against the yen, the U.S. automobile companies promptly raise their prices too. The strategy typical of the giant monopolistic corporations that now dominate our economy is to take advantage of increases in productivity to expand profits and/or intensify sales promotion, *not* to cut prices.

In short, whatever may have once been the case, the notion that higher labor productivity will help control inflation belongs in our time to the fantasy world of bourgeois economics. It has nothing to do with the real world of monopoly capital, least of all in the midst of the general stage of stagnation in which capitalism finds itself bogged down today.

What the Productivity Statistics Mean

We now turn to an examination of the measures of productivity that are supposed to demonstrate its declining rate of growth. On this it is important to be clear that the government's statistics (such

---

*Harry Magdoff, "A Note on Inflation," *Monthly Review*, December 1973, p. 23.
†*Ibid*, p. 24

as shown in Table 11-1 above) purport to measure output per man-hour for the *entire* private (non-government) economy. All private productive activity is intended to be covered—the output not only of factories, mines, and farms but also of massage parlors, movie studios and theaters, night clubs, charitable foundations, private schools and hospitals, supermarkets, banks, and real estate agencies.

Apart from everything else, the purely technical problems of arriving at a quantitative measure of this hodgepodge of goods and services are enormous. In essence what the statisticians do is add up the costs of production (including profits) and then adjust the totals by means of price indexes to arrive at a measure of production. This process involves a great deal of estimation (or guesswork) and leaves room for a large margin of error both in the total figure at any one time and in the amount of change from one period to another. But to enter now into a discussion of the technical shortcomings of these numbers would only serve to divert attention from the more important question of what they mean.

What needs to be understood is that these data do not take any account of the *quality* of the output; at best, they measure only quantity. Significant as this omission may be in the measurement of goods production, it is especially serious in the case of services. For example, the productivity of educational institutions rises as the class load for teachers is increased. But at the same time the quality of education is bound to decline since each teacher has to deal with more pupils and can devote less time and attention to each one. Are teachers then producing more or less? Similarly, the closing down of the only hospital in a neighborhood and the transfer of patients to a hospital in a distant area may appear to boost the productivity of the remaining hospital workers, but at the cost of the quality of medical services. Measures of quantitative output in these and other service occupations are of necessity biased and can only have an ambiguous and limited significance.

There are of course activities in the services field where productivity has a fairly clear-cut meaning. This is so, for example, of the routinized clerical work in banks and insurance companies. On the other hand, there are very large areas in which many millions of workers are engaged, where questions of definition of output cast doubt on the meaning of productivity measures and therefore also on the inferences that can be drawn from changes in such statistics.

But that is not all. A further and in some ways more serious difficulty arises from the practice of trying to arrive at an overall measure of the productivity of *all* types of private economic activity. The reason for this is that output-per-man-hour trends in goods production and in services behave very differently. In the former the nature of production allows for extensive mechanization and hence for constant improvements and changes designed to simplify and routinize the labor process, reducing the quantity of labor required. In services, too, the use of machinery is growing, but on the whole it is limited by the very nature of the service functions. For this reason the growth of productivity in goods production is bound to be much faster than in services.

The fact that productivity rises more rapidly in one sector than in another would by itself not be especially significant *if*—and this is a big *if* indeed—there were no change in the relative importance of the two sectors. But what if, say, the production of goods were rising more rapidly than the production of services? Then the higher growth rate of productivity in goods production would pull up the overall rate. And conversely a growing relative importance of services would pull down the overall rate. Thus, even if there is no change in productivity trends in either sector, the fact that one grows relative to the other will introduce changes in the overall index of productivity.

And it is precisely this type of distortion that underlies and in fact dominates the statistics now being used in the outpouring of propaganda about allegedly lagging productivity. The relevant facts are given in Tables 11-2 and 11-3. In Table 11-2 (p. 122), changes in employment for selected years since 1950 have been grouped into three categories: goods producing industries, services, and government.* Government is included in order to present a more complete picture of the employment situation.

---

*Transportation and public utilities are included under goods production. The reason for this is that even though the output of these industries is non-tangible, a significant portion is directly used in goods production. In any case, employment in this borderline group of industries is less than 6 percent of total employment, so that even if these sectors were classified under services neither the statistics nor the conclusions to be drawn from them would be significantly affected.

Table 11-2
Employment By Type of Industry

	Total	Goods-Producing Industries[a]	Service Industries[b]	Government[c]
			millions employed	
1950	52.3	29.7	16.6	6.0
1960	59.7	29.9	21.4	8.4
1970	74.4	31.6	30.2	12.6
1978	89.0	33.5	40.0	15.5

(a) Includes employment in agriculture, manufacturing, mining, construction, transportation, and public utilities. The data on agriculture are constructed on a different basis from those of the other industries in this table. Except for agriculture, these statistics include only wage and salary workers and are based on reports from the employing establishment. The data for agriculture include self-employed farmers as well as wage laborers, and the information is obtained from the monthly Labor Department field reports on employment and unemployment. Despite these differences, we believe that the above comparison fairly represents the basic differences in the trends of the three major divisions depicted.
(b) Includes employment in wholesale and retail trade, insurance, finance, real estate, and all other services.
(c) Includes employment in federal, state, and local government agencies.
Source: Economic Report of the President, January 1979 (Washington, D.C.: U.S. Government Printing Office, 1979).

Our attention, however, is focused on employment trends in the private sector. And there we can see a dramatic difference between changes of employment in goods production and in services. Employment in the former industries increased by only 3.8 million between 1950 and 1978, while employment in the latter grew by 23.4 million in the same period. From 1970 to 1978, the years in which productivity was presumably slowing down, employment in service activity increased more than five times as much as in the goods-producing industries (9.8 million compared with 1.9 million).

This big shift is further illustrated in Table 11-3. There we examine the changes in the distribution of employment in the private sector alone. And what we find is that the share of private employment in goods production declined steadily from 64 per-

Table 11-3
Percent Distribution of Employment in Private Industry

	Total	Goods-Producing Industries	Service Industries
1950	100.0	64.1	35.9
1960	100.0	58.3	41.7
1970	100.0	51.1	48.9
1978	100.0	45.6	54.4

Source: Same as Table 11-2.

cent of the total in 1950 to about 46 percent in 1978. On the other hand, service employment jumped from roughly 36 percent of the total in 1950 to over 54 percent in 1978.

What this all adds up to is that the productivity statistics for the entire private economy obscure what is happening. The important development is not declining rates of growth of productivity as such, but a shift in the relative number of jobs away from the areas of rapid productivity growth to areas of slower growing output per man-hour.* And these changes are due to the very nature of monopoly capitalism.

Monopolistic corporations compete by devoting an increasing amount of their resources, directly or indirectly, to sales promotion and distribution. In addition, the financial sector expands and becomes increasingly active in an incessant struggle to suck up an ever larger share of the surplus value produced elsewhere in the economy. Thus, more than one-half of the 10.2 million increase in service employment from 1970 to 1978 took place in wholesale and retail trade, and in finance, insurance, and real estate. Moreover, trade and many of the services act as a sponge for a large part of the reserve army of labor—in particular, Third World people, women, and undocumented aliens. It is there that the lowest-paying, temporary, and part-time jobs are to be found.

---

*For present purposes we are assuming that the official figures of productivity are reliable and meaningful measures. But, as noted above, this is a highly dubious assumption.

Rather than a slowdown in productivity causing inflation, as our bourgeois savants fear, it is inflation that is pushing women seeking to supplement family income to cope with a spiraling cost of living into the low-productivity and low-wage areas of trade and services.

Productivity in Manufacturing

The relatively slow growth of employment in goods production shown in Table 11-2 is of course due to a persistent increase in manufacturing productivity, faster in some years, slower in others. Declines do occur on rare occasions, but they are generally associated with some shock to the system as a whole such as war or depression. In Table 11-4 we can observe the annual changes in

Table 11-4
Production, Man-hours, and Productivity in Manufacturing Industries
1967 = 100

	Production	Man-hours worked	Productivity (output per man-hour)	Annual changes in productivity (percent change)	
1967	100.0	100.0	100.0		
1968	106.4	101.9	104.4	+4.4	
1969	110.0	103.7	106.1	+1.6	
1970	106.4	97.6	109.0	+2.8	Average
1971	108.2	94.2	114.9	+6.2	4.0
1972	118.9	98.5	120.7	+5.0	
1973	129.8	103.6	125.3	+3.8	
1974	129.4	101.7	127.2	+1.5	
1975	116.3	91.7	126.8	−0.3	Average
1976	129.5	96.5	134.2	+5.8	2.3
1977	137.1	100.3	136.7	+1.9	
1978	145.6	104.0	140.0	+2.4	

Source: The basic data from which this table was computed are given in the *Economic Report of the President, January 1979* (Washington, D.C.: U.S. Government Printing Office, 1979). The production index used is the Federal Reserve Board's. The man-hours index was derived by multiplying manufacturing employment by the average hours worked per week. The productivity index was calculated by dividing the production index by the man-hour index.

U.S. manufacturing productivity since 1967. The uneven pattern of growth stands out, and there is one year (1975) of actual decline obviously reflecting the sharp recession of 1974–1975.

Now the interesting thing from our present point of view is that the uneven pattern of growth gives statisticians a chance to play a game of comparing rates of growth in different periods. As demonstrated in the table, it is possible by breaking the period 1967–1978 into two subperiods (1967–1973 and 1974–1978) to "prove" that the rate of growth of productivity had fallen by almost half in the last few years—i.e., from an average of 4 percent to 2.3 percent. But when the statisticians and government pundits make such a comparison they totally ignore (or conveniently forget) the similar decline in the growth of production. In general, there is a logical correlation between increases in production and in productivity, with productivity speeding up as production accelerates and slowing down as production growth is retarded. And that is exactly what happened in recent years. The average annual increase in manufacturing production between 1967 and 1973 was 5 percent while the corresponding average from 1973 to 1978 was 2.4 percent. To the extent that there was a drop in the *increase of manufacturing productivity* it is merely a reflection of the severity of the 1974–1975 recession and the consequent retardation in the growth of manufacturing production.

Rather than play the game of juggling averages for selected years, it is vastly more important, from both analytical and social viewpoints, to attempt to grasp the significance of the entire period depicted in Table 11-4. For then we learn that from 1967 through 1978 man-hours of employment hardly changed at all, while production forged ahead. In some of these years man-hours actually declined while the production curve continued upward. Over the twelve-year period as a whole, it took only 4 percent more man-hours to produce a 46 percent increase in manufacturing output. Imagine how much more unemployment there would be today if productivity had gone up faster than it did! And what is the outlook for employment and unemployment in the future if, as our country's leaders demand, productivity increases do indeed speed up?

Is Greater Productivity Really Necessary?

We cannot end this examination of the current phoney campaign about sluggish productivity gains without at least raising the truly fundamental question: Why do we need more productivity? If we were talking about a Third World country, the answer would be obvious. There productive capacity in field and factory is woefully inadequate to meet the basic needs of the people. Because of that, a socialist country, or one striving to achieve socialism, would have to commit itself not only to provide jobs for all, but also to increase the capacity of workers to produce more.

But what about an industrially advanced country like the United States? Here we have a skilled labor force and an enormous productive capacity. If still more productive capacity should be needed, we have the knowledge and the means to create it—witness what happened during the Second World War. Yet despite all this available and potential wealth we have mass unemployment and poverty. Moreover, in addition to the army of unemployed, there are many millions presently engaged in wasteful and anti-social work who could be transferred to more useful productive activity. In view of the extent of our idle and wasted humanpower and of our enormous productive capacity, we surely don't need enhanced productivity to produce even much more than we are now producing. We have the productivity and the resources, in fact, to produce all that would be needed to eliminate poverty and provide everyone with fuller and richer lives.

Why then the desperate cry from Washington and the business community for ever greater productivity? The answer of course is to satisfy the crazy rationality of capitalism. An unrelenting growth in productivity is needed for one and only one purpose in this country: to enable capitalists to make greater profits and accumulate more capital. And since this necessity is so deep-rooted in the everyday operations of advanced capitalism, it has become enshrined as a cardinal myth of the ruling ideology.

It is about time to recognize the emperor's nakedness. The truth is that a rational society in the United States—one concerned with the people's needs and with the conditions under which they spend their working lives—would be more concerned with *reducing* than increasing productivity.

12.
Inflation Without End?

The U.S. economy has once again entered a recession which is accompanied by rampant inflation. The total output of goods and services, as measured by the Gross National Product (GNP), started to decline during the second quarter of this year. Prices, on the other hand, shot up at an annual rate of 10 percent during the same period. This behavior is typical of the recessions of the 1970s.

In earlier post-Second World War recessions (1948–1949, 1953–1954, and 1957–1958), prices on the whole remained fairly level, falling or rising by small amounts. Even this pattern already represented a break with the past, when depressions and recessions usually triggered a strong downward slide in prices. But the war in Vietnam, devaluations of the dollar, an explosion of debt, and creeping stagnation combined to bring about great changes in the operations of U.S. capitalism. A slump in output and employment no longer sufficed to stem the tide of inflation even for a brief period. Prices advanced by over 5 percent during the relatively mild recession of 1970. Then during the more severe and longer downturn between the end of 1973 and early 1975, prices moved up by at least 14 percent. And now, in the last recession of the decade, this seemingly contradictory pattern is again showing up in full force.

It is not that the inflation of the current decade or that of the post-Second World War period as a whole is an entirely new phenomenon. This can be seen from the accompanying chart which traces the movement of the annual wholesale price index calculated by the Bureau of Labor Statistics from 1900 to the

This article originally appeared in the November 1979 issue of *Monthly Review*.

present. We have added the broken line to highlight the trend up
to the end of the 1960s. This trend line clearly shows the dominant upward thrust of prices since the turn of the century.

There were, however, two major departures from the trend
line before 1970. First there was the burgeoning inflation induced by the First World War and its aftermath. The sharp 1921
depression, however, pricked that balloon, though even so prices
remained considerably higher than the prewar level. The Great
Depression produced the second and much more severe divergence from the long-term trend. This time prices were brought
down to the prewar level. Nevertheless, the gradual economic
recovery of the 1930s followed by the impact of the Second World
War raised the price level back to the historic trend. The long
postwar economic expansion then put prices on an upward course,
conforming with the overriding tendency of the century. This
lasted into the 1960s when the stimulus of the Vietnam War
initiated the new phase of rapid price increases which has been
with us ever since. Whether this represents a third and major
divergence from the historic trend line, or whether it is the
beginning of a whole new trend remains to be seen. In any case,
the rapid acceleration of price increases in the 1970s, though not
the fact of a rising price level as such, is clearly shown on the chart.
Whereas wholesale prices increased nearly 300 percent in the first
six decades of the twentieth century, they shot up by almost 90
percent in only the next nine years.

Before we look further into the current situation, it is important to be aware that the long-run trend of prices in this
century stands in sharp contrast to price behavior in the nineteenth century. Prices did of course fluctuate rather wildly at
certain junctures during the 1800s, especially in wartime. But
these inflationary periods were followed by deflations during
which prices sank back to pre-inflationary levels and then continued to drift downward. The dominant trend was the reverse
of what we observe in the chart. Thus, despite a rise in the
last years of the nineteenth century under the stimulus of the
Spanish-American War, the average price level for the 1890s as
a whole was 27 percent below that of the 1820s, the early years
of industrialization.

Wholesale Price Indexes
1967 = 100

Source: U.S. Bureau of Labor Statistics Data for 1979 are based on first six months of the year.

Why this big difference between the nineteenth and twentieth centuries? In our opinion, the answer is simple: the transformation of capitalism from the competitive stage of the nineteenth century to the monopoly stage which has dominated the twentieth century. In the former, lower production costs, achieved through mechanization and other productivity-increasing methods, were reflected in price reductions. In those days, price-cutting was a major weapon in the competitive struggle for market shares and increased profits. And that is why prices, especially of manufactured goods, drifted downward in the nineteenth century.

The intense competition of the earlier capitalist phase, however, led to its opposite. Many enterprises lost out in the struggle: some disappeared entirely, while others were merged with or bought up by financially stronger rivals. As a result, over time more and more industries came under the domination of relatively few giant corporations. The power thus amassed by the successful firms made it possible for them to gain and control markets by means other than price-cutting (a dirty word in the lexicon of Big Business). As price-cutting lost favor and gave way to price-boosting as a more effective road to larger profits, the downward price trend of competitive capitalism disappeared, to be replaced by the rising price trend which, as we have seen, has been a basic characteristic of the whole period of monopoly capitalism.

In normal times, the price-setting strategy of rival giant firms generally takes the following form:

> If one seller raises his price, this cannot possibly be interpreted [by a competitor] as an aggressive move. The worst that can happen to him is that the others will stand pat and he will have to rescind (or accept a smaller share of the market). In the case of a price cut, on the other hand, there is always the possibility that aggression is intended, that the cutter is trying to increase his share of the market by violating the taboo on price competition. If rivals do interpret the initial move in this way, a price war with losses to all may result. Hence everyone concerned is likely to be more circumspect about lowering than raising prices. Under oligopoly [few sellers], in other words, prices tend to be stickier on the downward side than on the upward side, and this fact introduces a significant upward bias into the general price level in a monopoly capitalist economy. There is

truth in *Business Week's* dictum that in the United States today the price system is one that "works only one way—up."*

Of course the corporations of the monopoly period are not all-powerful: the devastating effect of the Great Depression on their prices and profits was the clearest illustration of the limits within which they operate. But even so, they came through fairly well, suffering relatively few bankruptcies (partly, to be sure, because of government rescue efforts). And in the merger movements following the Second World War they increased their weight in the economy as a whole and fortified their market positions, with the result already commented on that price declines in postwar recessions have been small and most recently have disappeared altogether. It is symptomatic of the present situation that even when the corporate giants are caught with enormous inventories of unsold goods, as in the automobile industry during the last six months, they resort to discounts and rebates in order to increase sales, carefully refraining from reducing their list prices. These are strictly temporary sales-promotion devices and in no way interfere with price increases on new models. For example, at the very time when the media are full of advertisements by all the auto companies touting their rebate programs, the *New York Times* of October 2 carries a small item buried in its financial section with the headline, "G.M. and A.M.C. Raise 1980 Prices."

While most prices nowadays are strongly resistant to downward pressure, the pattern on the upside is quite different: a prolonged period of rising prices engenders a momentum of its own. What are prices for many sellers are costs for buyers, so that price increases end up as higher costs; and labor costs go up to the extent that workers are successful in their unending struggle to keep their real wages from being eroded. And so the scene is set for another round of price hikes, with each additional round planting the seeds for still another one, providing only that the government and financial institutions are ready to supply enough

---

*Baran and Sweezy, *Monopoly Capital* (New York: Monthly Review Press, 1966), p. 62.

funds, through the expansion of debt, to sustain the higher price-and-wage structure. But this too feeds the flames, because of the rising costs of financing the debt.

It is against this background that the upsurge of prices in the 1970s must be evaluated. The extent and timing of the acceleration is summarized in Table 12-1.

Table 12-1

	Average Annual Percent Increase in Prices
1952–67	2.0
1968–73	5.0
1974–79	7.8

Note: The price indexes used here are the "deflators" designed to estimate real changes in the GNP. Their advantage is that they take into account wholesale prices as well as consumer prices. The basic data to 1978 can be found in the *Economic Report of the President* (Washington, D.C.: Government Printing Office, 1979). The 1979 data are based on the first half of the year and can be found in the monthly issues of the *Survey of Current Business.*

During the 15 years 1952–1967 prices rose at an average annual rate of 2 percent, in some years a bit more and in others less. The first sign of an acceleration showed up with the beginning of the Vietnam War: the average annual rate of increase in 1965 and 1966 was 50 percent higher than the average for the 15-year period as a whole (3.1 vs. 2 percent). And this speed-up has gathered momentum from 1967 right up to the present. The price increases in *every* year since 1967 were higher than in *any* of the years between 1952 and 1967.

As we see it, three major, and in some ways interrelated, factors combined to set off the acceleration of the price spiral. The first and most important stimulus was the one already alluded to: the strains put on the economy by the prolonged and exhausting war in Vietnam. Added to this was the breakdown of the Bretton Woods international monetary system followed by two devaluations of the dollar in 1971. Apart from other effects, these devaluations (as well as those that have occurred in more recent years) raised the prices of imported raw materials and other goods that enter into the domestic price structure. Finally, the forces that fed the long post-Second World War prosperity period began to peter out in the late 1960s, paving the way for a new stage of stagnation. The response of the U.S. economy to this creeping stagnation was to foster a vast explosion of debt which, at least for the time being, served to shore up the demand for goods and services. At the same time, the ever-expanding debt required more and more of the same to enable business and consumers to service the debt already incurred and to stave off a potential collapse of the whole bloated credit system.

Table 12-2

	Average Annual Additions to Debt in 1972 Prices (billions of $)
1952–67	65.5
1968–73	133.5
1974–79	193.3

Source: Federal Reserve Board, *Flow of Funds Accounts,* various issues. The price index used to convert the figures into 1972 dollars was the Gross National Product implicit price deflator.

Table 12-2 presents a summary of the average annual additions to government, business, and consumer debt. The figures are adjusted to remove the effect of price changes. Therefore the increases shown for the same time-spans as in Table 12-1 are comparable from period to period. What is especially noteworthy here is that the pattern of the two step-ups in the growth of debt resembles that of the annual price increases in Table 12-1. In this case, the rate of increase of debt during 1968–1973 is 104 percent above that of the preceding period. And then during the 1974–1979 years the net additions to debt jump by another 45 percent.

Perplexed by this complex of developments, commentators in the bourgeois press as well as orthodox economists keep on looking for external evils on which to pin the blame for each new leap in prices: a drought in Africa, large Russian wheat purchases, a decrease in Peru's anchovy catch (used for animal feed), and, over and above all, soaring oil prices. There is no question that at one time or another unexpected disturbances do affect a part of the price system. But neither singly nor in combination can these special factors explain the historical record; not even the huge advance in oil prices posted by the OPEC countries at the end of 1973. For, as can be seen from Table 12-1, the acceleration of price increases began before 1974, when the new OPEC price schedule began to take full effect; from 1967 to 1973 the average annual price increase was two-and-a-half times that of the preceding 15 years. The truth is that the OPEC price hike has to be seen largely as a *response* to the long-lasting and accelerating rise in the prices of the commodities these countries buy from the United States and other advanced capitalist countries. The increase in oil prices did of course contribute to the speed-up in the general price level, especially after 1973, but it was part of the process and not the initiating cause.

In this connection, we should also clear the air on the role of wage increases as a causal factor. Part of the conventional wisdom is that recent inflation is the product of a conflict between monopolistic trade unions and giant corporations for a bigger share of a pie that isn't growing fast enough to satisfy both of them. But what are the facts? Table 12-3 summarizes data on average weekly earnings of production and non-supervisory workers, adjusted for changes in the cost of living. The first column shows gross average weekly earnings, and the second column presents estimated spendable earnings of a worker with three dependents (i.e., gross earnings less the federal income and social-security taxes a worker with three dependents would pay).

Here we see that real earnings increased between 1952 and 1967 at a rate of less than 2 percent a year. In that period of relatively mild inflation workers were ahead of the game, but clearly not by much. Gains in real wages were also achieved in the next period, from 1967 to 1973. But these gains slowed down (to about 1.2 percent a year) just when prices took a great leap forward. Now look at what happened in the years from 1973 to 1979, precisely the period of most rapid price acceleration. As might be expected, this was when workers' real wages were going

Table 12-3
Weekly Earnings of
Production and Nonsupervisory Workers
(in 1967 dollars)

	Gross Earnings	Spendable Earnings
1952	76.29	72.79
1967	101.84	90.86
1968	103.39	91.44
1973	109.26	95.73
1974	104.57	90.97
1975	101.67	90.53
1976	103.40	91.79
1977	103.93	93.48
1978	104.25	92.50
1979 (first half)	102.15	90.72

Source: Survey of Current Business, various issues. Spendable earnings are what a worker with three dependents would have left over after paying federal income and social security taxes.

down, the sharpest drop occurring between 1973 and 1975. There was some recovery after that, but note that in no year since 1973 did real gross earnings ever re-attain the previous peak. The plain fact is that real gross weekly earnings in the first half of 1979 were almost 7 percent below the 1973 high, and spendable earnings were 5 percent below. Real gross weekly earnings in the first half of 1979 were even below the level of 1968! (This does not mean of course that consumer demand as a whole declined, since self-employed professionals as well as those who live off surplus value are also consumers. In addition the consumption demand of the working class itself is sustained by the trend toward more women entering the labor force and by an increased use of consumer credit.)

As we emphasized above, the factor underlying the long-run upward price trend in this century has been the growing importance of monopoly capital. This does not mean of course that every increase or unusual acceleration of prices is directly due to the behavior of monopoly capitalists. But while monopoly capital may not be the direct cause of major upward movements of prices, it is nevertheless the necessary condition for their occurrence. Thus while the proximate cause of the most recent flare-up is the expansion of purchasing power through the virulent growth of private and public debt, it is because of the monopolistic structure of the economy that this added purchasing power goes into increasing prices rather than output. If monopoly is not the motor, it is nonetheless the *sine qua non* of the extraordinary inflation of the current decade as well as of the preceding upward spirals.

It is especially important to understand this because of the deeply ingrained myth that the market place is or could be the rational and even-handed regulator of economic affairs. The truth is quite the opposite. The market is indeed rational in the sense that it serves the aims of a profit-directed economy: to reproduce and strengthen the centers of monopoly power and to allocate resources in favor of the rich. But for others, and above all for those whose only source of livelihood is the sale of their labor power, the market is and always has been an engine of exploitation and repression.

This is becoming increasingly evident as the political agents of the ruling class try to maneuver between the Scylla of still more inflation and the Charybdis of a devastating depression. Whichever way it goes, workers are bound to be squeezed and to suffer. Their only recourse, as we believe more and more of them are beginning to recognize, is to organize and fight for their class interests. And this, as they will sooner or later discover in the course of the struggle, means not trying to do better for themselves within the framework dominated by market forces, but scrapping that framework altogether in favor of one capable of serving the interests of the entire society of producers.

13.
Whither U.S. Capitalism?

In one sense the answer to this question is that U.S. capitalism is going the way of the world capitalist system. It follows that some understanding, or at least assumption, about this is necessary to any intelligent discussion of the question. I will therefore begin by very briefly summarizing my own view of where the world capitalist system is going.

Considered as a global system, or at least the embryo of one, capitalism started in Western Europe in the fifteenth and sixteenth centuries. Its expansion continued with some ups and downs until the early twentieth century. The turning point, marking the end of this centuries-long expansion, came with the First World War and the Russian Revolution; and further setbacks were suffered as the result of the Second World War and the Chinese Revolution. By the middle of the twentieth century the countries with respectively the largest land area and the largest population had defected from the system. A number of others in Eastern Europe, Asia, the Caribbean, and Africa have done likewise. I do not believe that it is correct to speak of an alternative or rival global system, but capitalism has certainly suffered serious losses; and its possibilities of expansion, at least geographically and demographically, have been curtailed compared to what they were, or seemed to be, before 1914.

Nevertheless, and despite these very real losses and setbacks, it would be going too far to say that global capitalism actually went into a decline at that time. In fact it still covers well over half the

This is the text of a lecture delivered in Tokyo under the auspices of the Iwanami Shoten publishing house and published in the Japanese magazine *Sekai*. It appeared in the December 1979 issue of *Monthly Review*.

world's area and population. And the countries composing it—consisting of a core or center of a few advanced industrial nations and a periphery of a much larger number of basically dependent and less developed or underdeveloped ones—enjoyed an unprecedented period of expansion and prosperity (by capitalist standards) in the quarter century after the Second World War.

That this period has now come to an end is a view shared by many people of varying political and ideological persuasions. The marked slowdown in average rates of growth accompanied by high and in some cases even rising inflation, both characteristics of the last five or six years, are not normal capitalist phenomena. Other ominous developments have been the enormous expansion of debts at both national and international levels, the growing instability of the international monetary system, the resurgence of protectionism in various forms, and a skyrocketing increase in the price of gold and other commodities thought to be relatively safe repositories of value. These are all signs that the global capitalist system has entered a time of troubles from which there is no obvious escape route.

I agree with this diagnosis but would immediately add that a time of troubles—the term, I believe, was coined by historians of the decline of the Roman Empire—even a lengthy one punctuated by severe crises and dislocations is not equivalent to collapse. Social systems in fact do not collapse. They may weaken, decline, disintegrate—history provides many examples. But the only way they can disappear is through being replaced by another social system or systems. And this is usually a prolonged process which goes through many stages. To judge from historical experience, the time span involved should be thought of in terms of centuries rather than years, decades, or even generations.

I think it is plausible and even probable that the period we are now in—the last quarter of the twentieth century—marks a true turning point in the history of capitalism in the same sense that the period 1915–1950, embracing two world wars and two major revolutions, constituted a turning point. That earlier period was when capitalism reached the end of its rise as a world system. Now is the time when it begins to decline.

I do not want to speculate on how long this process of decline will last beyond saying that it will certainly be a long time—say, a hundred years or more if that helps you to keep things in perspective. Nor do I want to speculate on what will ultimately take capitalism's place. As I already noted, it has already suffered major defections. But these post-revolutionary societies are still of relatively recent origin, and there is not much agreement, even among observers who share the same ideology, about their basic nature or where they are going. All we need to say for present purposes is that further defections of a similar kind are not only possible but probable and should be looked upon as an integral aspect of the whole process of capitalist decline.

This, I think, is the overall context within which the question "Whither U.S. Capitalism?" can be usefully discussed. First of all I do not think it at all likely that the United States is a candidate for early defection from the capitalist system. The pattern of these defections up to now suggests that they tend to take place not in the center where the system is strong but in the periphery where it is weak. This of course is not what Marx and Engels expected, but it is clearly in line with the conclusion Lenin drew from the experiences of the First World War and the Russian Revolution, i.e., that imperialism (his name for the global capitalist system) can be likened to a chain which most easily breaks in its weakest links.

Obviously the United States which was on the winning side in both world wars and emerged from the second one in a clearly hegemonic position is not a weak link. True, it has lost ground relative to the other advanced industrial countries in the last two decades, but it is still the most powerful single capitalist country and seems likely to remain such for the foreseeable future. Though the whole picture may change at a later stage in the process of capitalist decline, just now the most plausible assumption would seem to be that the United States will be one of the last countries to remain within the system.

What, then, are the big problems facing U.S. capitalism at the present stage of the decline of the global system? And what strategies and policies are likely to be adopted to cope with these problems? I will discuss them under two headings, domestic and international, bearing in mind that these categories are to a considerable extent artificial and are imposed on reality for purposes of analysis rather than reflecting a non-existent clear-cut distinction.

Domestic. Under capitalism when conditions are favorable to the accumulation of capital and the process goes forward vigorously and with only minor interruptions, all the contradictions of the system are softened and the problems to which they give rise can either be solved or at least do not generate dangerous tensions and conflicts. Conversely when the accumulation process lags, all the contradictions grow more acute, the problems become more intractable, and the tensions and conflicts more dangerous. We are now in a period of the second kind, and its most prominent characteristic is the phenomenon which has come to be called stagflation.

As the term implies, stagflation consists of two parts: stagnation (persistent high levels of unemployment and excess capacity) and inflation. The stagnation part is the direct consequence of lagging capital accumulation, the inflation of pumping up demand through credit expansion and government fiscal and monetary policies. The apparent paradox that expansion of money demand can coexist with unemployment and idle productive capacity is explained by the prevalence of monopoly, oligopoly, and other forms of administered prices throughout the economy.

Keynes's theory of the way to manage the capitalist economy through a combination of monetary and fiscal policies assumed that so long as unemployed workers and unused productive capacity existed, expansion of effective demand would call forth increased output up to the point of full employment. But in a regime of noncompetitive prices, the increase in demand is met by *both* an increase in output *and* a rise in prices; and at a certain stage, which may be reached long before full employment, the price effect so far outweighs the output effect as to negate the effectiveness of the whole strategy. When this happens we have the phenomenon of chronic stagflation.

So far as the United States is concerned, and the same applies in varying degrees to other advanced capitalist countries, this has become in the last few years the normal state of the economy. It has to be added that once inflation has persisted for a number of years at rates which are high by historical standards, it tends to get structured into the system through the spreading efforts of wider and wider strata of the population to protect themselves against its damaging effects. When this happens, it becomes extremely difficult and perhaps impossible to check the process even by deliberately restrictive monetary and fiscal policies. In this situation—and I strongly suspect that it already exists in the United States—it may be that nothing short of a profound and prolonged depression would suffice to break the vicious cycle and halt the inflationary process.

There are of course many other domestic problems facing U.S. capitalism—energy; the physical and social decay of inner cities, manifesting itself in street crime, drug abuse, arson, and related pathological symptoms; persisting gaps between the incomes and opportunities open to whites and blacks and men and women; the list could be endlessly expanded. But they are all related in one way or another to stagflation, and there is no prospect that progress toward solving any of them could be achieved so long as stagflation dominates the economic and political scene as it now does. Domestically, therefore, stagflation must be considered *the* crucial issue around which struggles will take place to decide the direction U.S. capitalism is to follow in the period ahead.

International. I have already mentioned the growing instability of the international monetary system, and, as daily headlines keep reminding us, this is centered on the decline of the dollar vis-à-vis the currencies of the other developed capitalist countries. To understand why this is so important and what its implications are, we must recall a chapter in the recent economic history of the global capitalist system.

Emerging from the Second World War as the dominant capitalist power, the United States was able to impose on its defeated enemies and weakened allies a monetary system which officially recognized the dollar as universal money on a par (at $35 an ounce) with gold. The dollar became the unit of account for international trade and payments, and central banks held their reserves on which their national currencies were based in dollars as well as gold. As the world recovered from the war and entered into the unprecedented period of expansion already remarked upon, there emerged a pressing need for a growing supply of universal money; and since the supply of gold is necessarily very inelastic, this need could be met only by an increased flow of dollars from the United States into the banking systems of the rest of the world. This situation gave to the United States what has been called the "poisoned privilege" of spending more than it took in, i.e., to run a continuous deficit in its balance of payments, thus enabling it to command more and more of the world's resources without real cost. This arrangement was acceptable to all parties concerned so long as the outflow of dollars did not exceed the world's monetary need. But there was no mechanism to ensure such a correspondence of need and supply and, not surprisingly, the temptation for the United States to use the privilege to enhance its worldwide economic and military power was too strong to be resisted. So the outpouring continued on a rising scale, leading to the end of dollar/gold convertibility in 1971 and to the system of floating exchange rates in 1973. Since then things have gone from bad to worse. Greatly increased U.S. dependence on foreign oil plus two massive OPEC oil price hikes in 1973 and 1978 have vastly complicated the problems of inflation and the balance of payments: by now the dollar "overhang" (dollars held abroad and in effect constituting a claim on the United States) probably amounts to well over $800 billion. (The exact amount is not known because these so-called Eurodollars are not subject to any governmental control and their amount can be increased by the credit-creating activity of the banks in which they are held.)

The countries called upon to absorb this enormous outflow of dollars are placed in a difficult dilemma. They are well aware that dollars, like anything else in oversupply, are likely to lose in value; and if there is any inclination to forget, they are continually being reminded by the activity of private traders and speculators (including multinational corporations with huge cash resources) who, in their anxiety to avoid being trapped with unwanted dollars, exercise a more or less continuous downward pressure on dollar exchange rates. Central banks and treasuries would also like to reduce their dollar holdings; but they know that if they try to, they run the risk of undermining the value of their monetary reserves which are still largely in the form of dollars, and at the same time of destroying what is left of the international monetary system, with possibly disastrous consequences for all concerned. So these official agencies, instead of reducing their dollar holdings, have felt themselves obliged, more and more against their will, to go on increasing them by buying the dollars no one else wants to hold and in the process vastly expanding the supplies of their own currencies. The net result of all this has been what Robert Triffin, one of the world's leading experts on international monetary problems, has called "a fantastic increase in international liquidity" which "is undoubtedly the biggest factor in triggering the worst global inflation in history."*

The combination of domestic inflation and unremitting pressure on the dollar produced a sharp crisis at the end of October 1978, with the New York stock market dropping 100 points in two weeks and a near panic developing in the foreign-exchange markets. On that occasion the United States, acting in conjunction with its allies among the advanced capitalist countries, hastily put together a rescue operation for the dollar which succeeded in calming things down for a while but changed nothing fundamental. Now, a year later, events have reached a new climax. This time the first response of the United States has been to raise interest rates to unprecedented heights, hoping in this way to check both the domestic inflation and the decline of the dollar. The irony of the situation is that "success" in this effort would most likely mean turning what has so far been a mild recession into a deep depression.

It is too soon to judge whether this will in fact happen, but in any case it seems clear that the United States is headed for a major crisis, both domestic and international, far exceeding in scope and gravity anything experienced since the Second World War. Precisely what form it will take is impossible to guess, but it does seem likely that at some stage the government will be forced to intervene in a decisive way to prevent a slide into chaos. Likely forms of such intervention are: a freeze on prices and wages, a moratorium on debts, and imposition of rigid foreign-exchange

---

*Robert Triffin, "The International Role and Fate of the Dollar," *Foreign Affairs*, Winter 1978/79, p. 273.

controls. Actions of this kind of course would not solve anything, but they could mark a sharp break in the continuity of events and in this way initiate a new phase in the development of capitalism both in the United States and internationally. I believe this is the specific context in which the "Whither U.S. Capitalism?" question can be most fruitfully discussed.

It is worth stressing that the stock-market crash beginning in October 1929, just fifty years ago, did not constitute such a radical break. What it did was to announce the end of the prosperity of the 1920s and the beginning of a cyclical downturn. But hardly anyone at the time thought in terms of an economic collapse such as actually materialized and of the resulting crisis affecting the whole social structure. That came only later, in 1932–1933; and the real break marking the end of one era and the beginning of another was the closing of the country's banks after Roosevelt's accession to the presidency in the spring of 1933. The origin of the New Deal dates from then, not from the stock market crash of 1929.

Attempts to apply historical experience to the analysis of a current situation are risky but necessary, and I judge this to be especially true of the New Deal and the present. The differences between then and now are large and numerous: they constitute a clear warning to proceed with caution. And yet certain similarities seem to me both striking and fundamental. This is not so much true in the economic field as in the political. The economy has undergone extensive changes in the past half century. Stagflation was as yet completely unknown; the ratio of government spending to GNP was marginal compared to what it is today; some of the institutional reforms of the New Deal, like the legal status of unions, unemployment insurance, social security, and agricultural price supports, are now built into the economic structure; and the pile-up of debt, though impressive by the standards of the day, is dwarfed by what has occurred in the last decade. In the political sphere, on the other hand, the U.S. system has shown remarkable continuity and stability. The constitutional structure is pretty much what it was, and so are the identity, character, and role of the political parties. The problems, domestic and international, which have to be dealt with through the political process are bigger, more numerous, and more complicated, but the ways and means of coping have changed but little. This, I think, is an important clue to the present situation and what may come out of it.

The New Deal did not emerge full-blown out of the crisis of the spring of 1933. On the contrary, the first stage of the Roosevelt presidency gave rise to a business-oriented and business-dominated effort to cope with the catastrophic economic situation which had by then developed (unemployment in 1933 was about one quarter of the labor force, and the rate of capacity utilization was only a little over 50 percent). This was entirely in accord with the nature of the Democratic and Republican parties and the class forces they represented. The key measure was the National Industrial Recovery Act (NIRA) and the bureaucratic apparatus of industrial codes which it established. Business was in effect given *carte blanche* to organize monopolistic associations, a long-held ambition, while labor was thrown a sop in the form of unenforceable promises of the right to organize and bargain collectively, and agriculture was provided with a framework of production and price controls.

Given the desperate plight of workers, farmers, and petty producers at the time, this has to be considered a very minimal response to the situation. And in practice of course it turned out to be minimally effective. The business cycle hit bottom in 1933, but the ensuing recovery was very slow (unemployment was still at more than 20 percent of the labor force in 1934) and did little to alleviate mass suffering. The unemployed had nothing but soup kitchens and private charity to fall back on, and workers' efforts to defend themselves against rampant wage-cutting and deteriorating working conditions continued as in the past to be repressed by the courts and police.

It was in these circumstances, some four years after the stock market crash of 1929, that a real mass movement began to develop, which demanded concrete, effective measures to redress what had become an intolerable situation for literally tens of millions of people. Fortunately for the ruling class, which had failed its elementary responsibilities to society and was quite unprepared to take effective action, the man it had put in the White

House in 1932 and who had declared the bank holiday immediately on taking office in 1933, turned out to have the qualities of a great political leader. Sensing the potential of the gathering storm, Roosevelt—instead of tailing along behind the mass movement and running the risk of letting it get out of control—put himself at its head and steered it into what were from capitalism's point of view safe waters. This was the meaning of the New Deal—a reform movement powered from below and kept within acceptable bounds by Roosevelt and the large, but probably not majority, section of the ruling class which was farseeing enough to support him.

One more comment on the New Deal will suffice for present purposes. By 1936 it had reached its peak. The reforms that affected the popular masses—work relief, public works, unemployment insurance, social security, agricultural price supports, the Wagner Act—had begun to take hold; and the cyclical recovery which had begun in 1933 was in full swing. In the 1936 elections Roosevelt was resoundingly re-elected, carrying all but two of the then 48 states. For the first time since 1929 the outlook for the future seemed good. But the euphoria was short-lived. In late 1937 a new recession struck. Unemployment rose from the 1937 level of 14.3 percent to 19 percent in 1938. The New Deal had run out of reforms, and none of them, it seemed, had any effect on capitalism's basic contradiction, the tendency to overaccumulate and overproduce. All Roosevelt could do was establish a high-level Temporary National Economic Commission (TNEC) and give it the task of studying the economy and coming in with new recommendations. Fortunately for him and for U.S. capitalism, the TNEC and the problem it was supposed to solve were soon rendered obsolete as the Second World War and its aftermath took over and gave the system a new lease on life which only now, forty years later, seems to be running out.

In a very real sense the crisis faced by U.S. capitalism today is simply a resumption of the one which was interrupted and postponed by the Second World War. The heart of the matter then was stagnation; today it is stagnation combined with inflation and an enormously complicated international monetary and financial mess. The reforms introduced by the New Deal had already shown themselves powerless to cope with the problems of its own time. Today they are irrelevant, long since institutionalized and integrated into the functioning of the system. The country's political structure is totally incapable of acting effectively: its leaders do not even understand what is going on. About all they can do is institute emergency measures to check a slide into chaos. But after that, what?

I do not know, and I don't think anyone else does either. I can only speculate that the shock of panic and the fear of threatened chaos will release long-dormant political energies and lead fairly rapidly to a new constellation of political forces, as happened in 1933–1934.

If this is correct, one must expect a polarization toward the right and the left, some signs of which can already be detected. The right obviously will aim at a solution at the expense of popular living standards. The left's first concern will be defense against further cuts and perhaps attempts to recoup some of the losses suffered during recent years of aggravated inflation. But since even success along these lines would leave the basic problem untouched, it seems inevitable that the left will be forced to develop something in the nature of a comprehensive program designed to make the system work more in the interest of the lower-income groups, most of whom are wage-workers or unemployed.

It might seem that what I am describing is simply the setting for an intensified class struggle between the capitalists and their upper-income allies on the one hand and the working class on the other. And in the light of U.S. history, especially the failure of the working class at any time, even during the New Deal, to build a viable political party of its own, it might also seem that the outcome of this struggle, at least for a long time to come, is foreordained.

Those who see things in this light—and there are many of them, even on the left—tend to the view that U.S. capitalism is headed toward an American version of the corporate state, authoritarian and repressive internally, increasingly militaristic and aggressive externally.

It seems to me, however, that matters are not quite so simple. There are at least two problems with this "solution" to the crisis of U.S. capitalism. First, it assumes that because the working class has never yet organized itself for effective independent political action it never will in the future either. In my view this reflects a simplistic view of the history of class struggles in the United States and quite unjustifiably rules out the emergence of new patterns of behavior and forms of struggle. Second, it assumes that the capitalists will be united behind a fascist-type policy of repression, and this seems to me doubtful too. Not only is a strategy of this kind costly to large elements of the middle and upper classes, as the whole history of fascism shows, but even more important, it is no solution at all to the real problems of U.S. capitalism. The basic disease of monopoly capitalism is an increasingly powerful tendency to overaccumulate. At anything approaching full employment, the surplus accruing to the propertied classes is far more than they can profitably invest. An attempt to remedy this by further curtailing the standard of living of the lower-income groups can only make things worse. What is needed, in fact, is the exact opposite, a substantial and *increasing* standard of living of the lower-income groups, not necessarily in the form of more individual consumption: more important at this stage of capitalist development is a greater improvement in collective consumption and the quality of life.

It follows that there is at least the objective basis for a cross-class alliance between those who suffer most from the system's crisis and the more far-seeing elements of the ruling class. This is similar to the situation that existed in 1933 and gave rise to the New Deal. But history never really repeats itself, and there is no need to assume that such an alliance would take the same form as it did half a century ago. The workers were very much the junior partner then. Do they have to be this time as well? The answer, in my opinion, depends not on logic or theory but on what actually happens in the course of the struggle. And that, I think, is not only what we *cannot* predict but *should not try* to predict. Better to join the struggle and try to affect its course. Not only the people of the United States but the peoples of all the world have an enormous stake in the outcome.

14.
Gold Mania—Capitalism's Fever Chart

The orgy of gold buying that pushed the price of gold up to well above $400 an ounce last autumn, and the subsequent hectic speculation that has kept the price fluctuating around that level, resembles the kind of mania that in the history of capitalism has often been the prelude to a major financial crisis. It would be a foolhardy and idle exercise to try to forecast the future course of the current speculative madness. What is important, rather, is to recognize that this drastic increase in the price of gold—now at a level more than ten times that of 1971—is a symptom, one might say a fever indicator, of the deepseated troubles facing the capitalist world. At a minimum, the recent behavior of the price of gold clearly demonstrates how quickly panic can overtake and shake up financial markets as the more sensitive sectors of the bourgeoisie become increasingly aware of the shoals lying ahead for the leading capitalist nations and for the international monetary system.

The linchpin of the international monetary system during most of the years since the Second World War was the maintenance of a fixed *dollar* price for gold. At the Bretton Woods Conference in 1944 it was agreed that gold would be valued at $35 per ounce in all official transactions. This was intended to provide a firm basis for foreign-exchange stability, which in turn would facilitate the flourishing of international trade. And despite many tensions and growing problems, the system worked fairly well until the early 1970s. True, the ability to maintain such a fixed price was at

This article originally appeared in the January 1980 issue of *Monthly Review*.

times threatened by speculation in the private gold markets, but in the main the leading capitalist nations were able to intervene sufficiently in those markets to prevent the price from reaching a level much above the magic $35. As for official transactions between central banks, the system functioned as planned so long as the United States was able and willing to live up to its commitment to convert, upon the request of foreign central banks, dollars into gold at the fixed price.

The postwar international monetary system got off to a good start because during most of the first two decades after the war the United States was in a clearly dominant position. At the end of the war the country was by far the leading manufacturer, foreign trader, international banker, and, last but certainly not least, global military power. At the same time most of the government-held gold of the capitalist world was in the vaults of the U.S. Treasury Department. The other capitalist nations, notably the countries devastated by war, had relatively little gold and were desperate for dollars to buy food, coal, and manufactured goods from the United States. Under such conditions, the enshrinement of the dollar as *the* international medium of exchange appeared to be a reasonable and logical substitute for the more traditional medium, gold.

In the corridors of power one could hear repeated with increasing frequency Keynes's put-down of gold as no more than a "barbarous relic." Who other than jewelers and dentists needed gold when the dollar was just as good, if not better, as an international means of payment? What was conveniently overlooked, especially by U.S. "experts," was that the power of the dollar was rooted in the hegemonic position of U.S. capitalism. The fact is that the dollar started to lose its luster just as soon as rival imperialist powers began to get back their strength and their giant corporations and banks once again became serious competitors in the international arena.

By that time, however, the contending imperialist powers were caught in a trap. At $35 per ounce there just wasn't enough gold in governmental (or central bank) coffers to finance the rapid expansion of international trade with its accompanying inflation of world prices. For this, alternative means of payment were urgently required. And, as it happened, the United States was happy to meet this need through flooding world markets with dollars to finance its military bases and imperialist wars; to buy control or influence over weaker nations with military and economic aid; and to facilitate the global expansion of its multinational corporations. When the United States needed more money to pay for these far-flung imperialist activities, it just created more dollars in the form of bank credits. But the more this swelling tide of dollars inundated the foreign banks, the less did these dollars glitter like gold. Gold, after all, is the undisputed repository of value in all markets. Dollars, on the other hand, are merely IOUs that are ultimately valuable only for the purchase of U.S. goods and services. Hence the dilemma for other countries and particularly for rival capitalist centers: in the short run the inflowing dollars were good for business; but, since they were only IOUs, the value of this vast and seemingly endless accumulation could at some time in the future collapse.

Foreign financiers had no easy way out of this bind. If they refused to accept dollars as the equivalent of gold, the entire international structure could come tumbling down. So they played by the established rules of the game, made as much profit as they could, and at the same time sought ways to evade them. As a hedge against a possible day of judgment, they kept on converting some of their dollar hoards into gold. The upshot was that the commitment made by the United States under the Bretton Woods Agreement to convert, upon request, foreign dollar assets into gold became an increasingly empty one. This can be seen in the following simple summary:

Table 14-1

End of	U.S. Gold Reserves	U.S. Dollars Held Abroad
	Billions of Dollars	
1955	21.8	11.7
1971	10.1	65.6

Source: Federal Reserve Bulletin, various issues.

Clearly, the U.S. pledge to exchange gold for dollars was plausible back in the 1950s when there was almost twice as much gold on hand as there were dollars abroad. But the continuous and ever larger U.S. balance-of-payments deficits that generated the pile-up of dollars abroad, together with the drying up of U.S. gold reserves, changed all that. The contradiction between the U.S. gold-conversion commitment and the possibility of living up to it kept on growing—until it reached a point of crisis in 1971. By that time, as can be seen from the above figures, the amount of foreign-held dollars was more than six times the U.S. gold reserves. And, facing up to that reality, the United States was forced to default: in August 1971 gold and dollars were declared no longer interchangeable, and the dollar was devalued.*

This unilateral action, soon followed by changes in the regulations of the International Monetary Fund (IMF), effectively removed the $35 lid on the price of gold. The "free" private market took over, and the price leaped upward, reflecting the impact of both the extensive postwar inflation and the devaluation of the U.S. dollar. Once let loose, the price of gold fluctuated widely, moving up toward the $200-per-ounce level by the end of 1974.

The sharp increase and wide fluctuations, however, posed new obstacles to the IMF's aim to maintain some reasonable order in the international monetary system. On the one hand, it had proved impossible to maintain a fixed price for gold as the anchor of the system. On the other hand, gold was still counted as a monetary reserve by the IMF and its members. Given this continued reserve role for gold and the evident desire of many countries to peg the international value of their currencies to gold, it was inevitable that wide fluctuations in the price of gold would be a constant source of disorder in foreign-exchange markets.

The decision was therefore reached by the IMF at the beginning of 1976 to demonetize gold: that is, to reduce and eventually eliminate the role of gold as a medium of international payments and as a currency peg. This step was fully consistent with the desires of the United States. For, despite the actual and poten-

---

*For a fuller discussion of the 1971 crisis see "The End of U.S. Hegemony," *Monthly Review*, October 1971.

tially even greater weakness of the dollar, it still remained by a wide margin the major reserve currency in the capitalist world. The further gold could be removed from the center of the stage, the more dependent would the rest of the world remain on the use of the dollar.

Once the speculators learned of the plan to demonetize gold, and especially when the IMF started to carry out its program by a measured reduction of its gold stock, the price of gold took a nose-dive. In 1976 the gold price sank by almost half from its previous high—to a price of approximately $108 per ounce. In view of what has been happening more recently in the gold market, it is important to understand that this kind of a decline is consistent with the ordinary rationality of the capitalist market place. The supply of gold offered for sale increased, speculative demand weakened in view of the official program to keep on selling the IMF's gold and to demonetize gold—and the price of gold consequently fell. Nevertheless, the drop of the *U.S. dollar price* of gold did not last long, giving way to sizable increases during 1977 and 1978. This again was "logical" in view of the rapid depreciation of the international value of the dollar in those years. (For this, see Chapter 3 of this volume.) At the same time, the price of gold in Swiss francs kept on declining throughout 1977 and until late 1978.

In contrast, the behavior of the gold market in 1979 displayed entirely new features. First, the price skyrocketed in spurts which the *Wall Street Journal* termed "near-hysterical." From September 1978 to August 1979 the price advanced by a little over 40 percent, from $210 to $300 per ounce. Then, in a little more than a month, from the end of August to October 2nd, it leaped upward by about 50 percent, from $300 to $447 per ounce.

Second, the rise in the price of gold in 1979 was no longer a simple response to a depreciating U.S. dollar. The gold price increased relative to *all* currencies. No more could the price gyrations be understood as a flight from the dollar. They were now the result of a flight from all the leading currencies: from the French, German, Swiss, and Japanese.

Finally, the upward price spiral was apparently in flagrant contradiction to the law of supply and demand. Throughout this period the IMF continued to sell gold. Then, in addition, the U.S. Treasury began in May 1978 to sell even larger quantities of gold in monthly auctions. Meanwhile, no significant changes took place in the customary gold requirements by industry and commerce. Accordingly, the normal expectation would be that the dumping of gold on the market would push the price down. Yet what happened was just the opposite. *The larger the quantity of gold offered for sale, the stronger demand grew, and the higher the price soared.*

A common explanation for this strange phenomenon is that speculators became wildly irrational. The new price level, however, would not have lasted as long as it has if it were merely the product of manipulation by market operators. Behind it had to be some solid basis of demand: individuals, businesses, and governments that were desperately anxious to build up their hoards of gold, and at unprecedentedly high prices. Behind this, no doubt, lies the conviction of central bankers and other financiers that despite, or perhaps because of, the mystical feature of gold, possession of this precious metal is the ultimate trustworthy medium of exchange in a world beset by seemingly endless inflation and instability of the international monetary system.

Here we need to keep in mind that as a result of the flood of U.S. dollars abroad and the maintenance for years of a lid on gold prices, the gold proportion of the reserves of central banks outside the United States had declined sharply while dollars had become the dominant form of reserves. With the new price level of gold, the situation is reversed: less than 24 percent of the reserves of the leading capitalist nations had formerly been in the form of gold at the old "official" price,* the rest of the reserves being in the form of foreign exchange, predominantly dollars; now, with the removal of an "official" price and the skyrocketing of the gold price, the proportion of the reserves held in gold, if measured in current prices, amounts to almost 60 percent (according to a tabulation by *The Economist,* October 27, 1979).

---

*After the U.S. devaluation of the dollar in 1971, the IMF raised the price at which central bank gold stock was to be valued to $42.22 per ounce. Then, in 1976, as part of the plan to demonetize gold, the IMF lifted its restrictions on how central banks should value their gold in settling accounts with each other.

Given this situation, the aim of U.S. monetary authorities to eliminate the monetary role of gold (and thereby strengthen the international role of the dollar) is and will remain mere wishful dreaming. *Business Week* (October 1, 1979) quoted a Paris banker who put the point in a nutshell:

> The United States has failed in its efforts to demonetize gold, and what is important is that previously the United States had always succeeded in imposing its views on this sort of monetary question. Now it can no longer do so.

It would clearly be in the interest of U.S. imperialism if gold would indeed be treated by the rest of the capitalist world as a "barbarous relic." But that would be possible only if we had passed the age of economic barbarism. No matter how much economists may rail against reliance on gold as an atavistic throwback, the fact remains that the only viable alternative to an "objective" regulator of the international monetary mechanism would be effective planning and genuine cooperation among the leading nations in the service of a theoretical common good. But this would entail a willingness on the part of all of them to make compromises involving sacrifice of their perceived self-interest, and if four centuries of capitalist history have demonstrated anything it surely is that no such behavior can be expected from societies organized as sovereign nation states. Indeed, experience suggests that the greater the degree of interdependence among capitalist nations, the greater is the need for each to protect its own interests at the expense of the others. And this of course generates not cooperation but competition and conflict which tend to disrupt the harmony of the international system and lead to recurrent periods of disorder.

To be sure, there have been interludes in the history of capitalism when there was more or less order in the economic relations among the advanced capitalist nations. But these have been periods when there was a clear-cut hegemony by one of the powers that could pretty much lay down the law, such as England during a large part of the nineteenth century and the United States in the first two decades after the Second World War. Now, since the decline of U.S. hegemony, a new era of international economic disorder has emerged, with the gyrations in the price of gold being one of its characteristic symptoms.

The troubles of capitalist societies, however, are internal as well as external. Although the extent of inflation varies from country to country, no country has escaped being infected with the disease. That, combined with a general state of lagging growth and a present or impending cyclical downswing, raises the specter of a world-wide major depression. In these circumstances, it is no wonder that the more nervous capitalist interests have been shifting part of their wealth into nonproductive gold. Seen in this light, the flight from paper currencies is both a product and symptom of the current deep-seated capitalist illness. As we go to press, panic once again seems to be seizing the gold market. This may of course subside, but the forces underlying it are still very much with us and, unless something entirely unexpected intervenes, seem certain to produce more and bigger panics of one sort or another in the period ahead.

15.
U.S. Foreign Policy in the 1980s

The trouble with most discussions of U.S. foreign policy, on the left as well as on the right, is that they are placed in a totally inappropriate framework of assumptions and preconceptions. The most important of these is that the United States and the Soviet Union are locked in a gigantic superpower struggle for world supremacy. This is seen as *the* number one contradiction in the world today to which all other contradictions and conflicts are subordinate. From this premise it is assumed to follow that a gain by either side is, directly or indirectly, a loss for the other. In other words, the superpowers are playing what is called a zero-sum game: a plus for one is cancelled out by a minus for the other; it is impossible for both to gain or lose at the same time.

Into this theoretical framework there is inserted an empirically observed trend, namely, that the curve of U.S. power and influence in the world has been declining ever since it reached an historic peak at the end of the Second World War. The obverse of this, derived from the underlying theory but rarely subjected to any sort of empirical scrutiny, is that the curve of Soviet power and influence has been rising during the same period. The supposed coexistence of these closely interrelated trends, taken to be the dominant characteristic of the whole postwar period, has gradually assumed the status of a self-evident axiom which forms the starting point of all reasoning about geopolitics and international relations.

The most consistent expression of this view is the well known Chinese doctrine—which clearly constitutes the actual premise of

This article originally appeared in the April 1980 issue of *Monthly Review*.

Chinese foreign policy—that there are two imperialisms in the world today, the American and the Russian, and that the former is in decline and on the defensive while the latter is in the ascendency and on the offensive. Exactly the same thought, though of course couched in different terms, has long figured in the shaping and execution of American policy, most notably in the aftermath of the Soviet invasion of Afghanistan. It is hardly an exaggeration to say that the reaction to this event in the United States*—at the governmental level as well as in the realm of public opinion—would be totally incomprehensible except in the context of this theory of the two imperialisms, one declining and one rising.

There are two basic flaws in this interpretation of the post-Second World War period. First, there is no reason for the *a priori* assumption that the superpower game is of the zero-sum variety. Logically they could both gain or lose at the same time: it is a question of fact, not of theory. And second, a serious examination of the record clearly points to the conclusion that during the last two decades *both* superpowers have in fact been losing power and influence. In the case of the United States this is obvious; indeed, as mentioned earlier, the decline begins much sooner, certainly no later than the collapse of the Chiang Kai-shek regime in China and the victory of the Communists in 1949. Interestingly, the decline in Soviet power and influence also begins with the "loss" of China, made definitive by the Sino-Soviet split of 1960. Since then the Soviet Union has had successes and failures in the international arena, but the failures have outweighed the successes and the overall trend has been down. This is the conclusion of a sober, factual investigation by the Washington-based Center

---

*A typical example of this reaction appears in a letter to the editor of the *New York Times* (March 12, 1980): "In his appearance before the Senate Foreign Relations Committee on Feb. 27, Ambassador George Kennan accused the Carter administration of overreacting to the Soviet invasion of Afghanistan. . . . The ambassador expresses concern over what he perceives as a developing war psychology. But surely he must recognize, better than most, that Russia's unimpeded advances have been encouraged by the perceived indifference and lack of will and capacity of the United States. Now we are at the point of recovering both our awareness and our resolve. We are starting to combine our resolve with that of others into an effective force for peace."

for Defense Information.* So important are the findings of this study that we reproduce here the complete summary as presented in the document itself:

Defense Monitor in Brief

• American fears of Soviet geopolitical momentum strongly affect U.S. foreign and military policy.

• A comprehensive study of trends of Soviet world influence in 155 countries since World War II does not support perceptions of consistent Soviet advances and devastating U.S. setbacks.

• Outside Eastern Europe, Soviet influence has lacked staying power. Inability to accumulate influence in foreign countries over long periods is a dominant feature of Soviet world involvement.

• Starting from a very low base of political, economic, and military involvement, the Soviets have increased their influence around the world. Starting with influence in 9 percent of the world's nations in 1945, they peaked at 14 percent in the late 1950s, and today have influence in 12 percent of the world's nations. Of the 155 countries in the world today, the Soviets have influence in 19.

• The Soviets have been successful in gaining influence primarily among the world's poorest and most desperate countries.

• Soviet foreign involvement has to a large extent been shaped by indigenous conditions, and the Soviets have been unable to command loyalty or obedience.

• Soviet setbacks in China, Indonesia, Egypt, India, and Iraq dwarf marginal Soviet advances in lesser countries.

• Temporary Soviet successes in backward countries have proved costly to the Soviet Union. They provide no justification for American alarmism or military intervention. U.S. policies should emphasize our non-military advantages in the competition for world influence.

The most significant of these conclusions is not the one relating to the number and proportion of countries in which the Soviet Union is judged to have influence but rather the next to the last item calling attention to the large and important countries in

---

*"Soviet Geopolitical Momentum: Myth or Menace—Trends of Soviet Influence Around the World from 1945 to 1980," *The Defense Monitor,* January 1980, published by the Center for Defense Information, 122 Maryland Ave., NE, Washington, DC 20022. Copies of this issue of *The Defense Monitor* can be obtained from Halcyon House, Inc., 67 Byron Rd., Weston, MA 02193 at $1 for single copies.

which the Soviet Union has *lost* influence during the last two decades. This record, on the face of it, is simply not compatible with the belief in a rising and aggressively successful Soviet imperialism. Nor is there any reason to believe that current efforts of the Soviet Union to expand its influence in such areas as Indochina, the Horn of Africa, and Southern Africa are meeting with significantly more success than similar efforts have achieved in the past.

It is very important to understand this, since it relates to the present and future rather than simply to what happened in the past. It is easy for the Soviet Union to get involved in almost any area of the Third World you may care to designate. In all of them without exception complex national and class struggles are in process. In terms of money and arms the contending forces are weak and needy, and the Soviet Union is an ample source of both. Political and ideological barriers prevent some of the contestants from approaching or accepting aid from the Soviet Union. This applies mainly to defenders of the status quo who find the United States a better and more congenial source of supply. But nationalist and revolutionary forces, whether on the offensive or defensive, rarely have scruples of this kind and eagerly accept Soviet aid, usually wihout giving or indeed being able to give anything concrete in return. The result is that the Soviet Union frequently gets into situations in which it plays an important role for a time but from which it derives no lasting benefit or influence and from which indeed it may be unable to extricate itself without serious economic and political costs.

A classic example of this kind is provided by the Horn of Africa. As long as Ethiopia was a U.S. client state, the Soviet Union gave aid to the Eritrean independence struggle and to Somalia which had territorial claims on Ethiopia's Ogaden area, in the latter case actually getting naval-base facilities and perhaps hoping for the same in Eritrea later on. But when Haile Selassie was overthrown by a popular upheaval, Moscow apparently decided it could gain more by shifting its support to the new nationalist regime in Ethiopia. The latter, once assured of Soviet support, rejected Soviet efforts to mediate the Eritrean conflict and instead launched an all-out war to crush the revolutionary Eritrean People's Liberation Front (EPLF), in the process dragging the Russians (and the Cubans who had unwisely followed the Soviet lead) deeper and deeper into a sordid counter-revolutionary adventure. Latest reports at the time of writing indicate that after initial setbacks for the Eritreans, the tide has turned in their favor and that the situation in Ethiopia is seriously deteriorating. Two British academics, returning from a recent visit to Eritrea, reported in the (London) *Guardian* (January 24, 1980):

> While the Soviet Union's invasion of Afghanistan has dominated world headlines, its attempts to direct affairs in the strategically more significant and economically more attractive Horn of Africa have passed almost unnoticed. Yet in the past month the Russian-backed Ethiopian army has suffered two serious blows from the guerrillas of the Eritrean People's Liberation Front.
>
> Striking out southwards and eastwards from their mountainous base area in the northern Eritrean province of Sahel, the EPLF forces have forestalled an Ethiopian pincer offensive designed to destroy them, and in the process have gone a long way towards restoring the military equilibrium lost in the "strategic retreat" of 1978. . . .
>
> Faced with a divided and demoralized army, the EPLF are now in a stronger position than at any time in the past 18 months. . . .
>
> Everything now points to the failure of the Dergue's [the ruling group in Ethiopia] ambitions in Eritrea. More than that the survival of Mengistu [head of the Dergue] regime itself is now in question. Armed struggles have erupted in three further provinces, most notably in Tigre. . . .
>
> Although Mengistu might not be their most dependable ally, the Soviet Union's overriding economic and strategic interest is still, as it was for the United States, a greater Ethiopia with direct access to the Red Sea. Mengistu's military solution remains their only option.

It looks as though Ethiopia may come to share the privilege so far monopolized by China as a country which has been "lost" twice, once by each of the superpowers.

For present purposes there is no need to analyze the Soviet position in Indochina or Southern Africa. Suffice it to say that the situations are very different, but that neither looks at all promising from the point of view of Soviet power and influence. Given a gravely weakened economy and debilitating entanglements in the affairs of its Cambodian and Laotian neighbors, Vietnam may cling for a long time to its alliance with the Soviet Union, but it is hard to see what strategic, let alone economic, benefits the Russians can expect to get out of it. From their point of view, the prospects in Southern Africa are certainly much more favorable. By helping the nationalist and revolutionary forces in Angola, Mozambique, and Zimbabwe, the Russians appear at their best before public opinion in the Third World and the international left generally. But it is something altogether different to claim or imply, as Americans and Chinese persist in doing, that the Russians are somehow penetrating the area and establishing permanent power positions. The truth is that after a century of ruthless colonial oppression, no genuine nationalist or revolutionary movement in Africa is going to settle for a new foreign overlord. To be sure, Africa still has a long way to go to gain economic independence, but that is a problem which concerns Africans and the traditional imperialist (mostly Western European) powers and in the solution of which the USSR is unlikely to play even a marginal role. The following summary figures on trade with Africa show how insignificant the Soviet Union is in Africa's economic affairs:

Table 15-1
Trade with Africa (excluding South Africa)
(imports plus exports — billions of dollars)

Western Europe	41.7
Japan	5.6
United States	7.3
USSR	1.6
Eastern Europe	1.9

Source: Africa News, March 28, 1977.

Why have we devoted so much space to the faltering role of the Soviet Union in world affairs? The answer is that unless this is understood and taken fully into account, it is impossible to uncover the real nature and meaning of U.S. foreign policy. This is not to discount the danger of a military confrontation between the United States and the Soviet Union. Both superpowers are equipped to blow up the world, and that situation will not change in the foreseeable future regardless of their relative positions of power and influence with respect to other countries. By the same token, neither can hope to improve its chances of winning an unwinnable nuclear war by gains in the international arena, nor will the security of either be significantly compromised by losses. If nevertheless both are intensely preoccupied by their power and influence in the world—as indeed they are—the explanation must be sought elsewhere than in the game of superpower rivalry.

Here we leave the Soviet Union and turn our attention to the United States. And what we find is that the United States is so thoroughly integrated into the global capitalist system as it has evolved under U.S. hegemony in the post-Second World War period that any changes, particularly if they are of a potentially cumulative character, threaten the viability of the U.S. economy in its present form and hence constitute a clear and present danger to the enormous wealth, power, and privileges of the business and financial elite which dominates the country's economic and political affairs. A full, up-to-date treatment of this theme would of course fill a book. Here we will focus on three key aspects: (1) direct foreign investment of U.S. multinational corporations; (2) the role of foreign investment in the country's balance of payments; and (3) the foreign involvement of U.S. banks.

Foreign Investment of Multinationals. In 1966 U.S. multinational corporations had $52 billion invested abroad, and this had grown to $168 billion by 1978 (the figures are for book value: market value would be much greater). This sizable increase was to a large extent achieved by the reinvestment of the earnings of foreign branches. It is important to recognize that the multinational corporations sent only $50 billion out of the United States. The total direct investment abroad, however, produced $203 billion of income for the multinationals during this period. Part of the income was reinvested abroad. But $132 billion came back to the United States in the form of dividends, interest, royalties, fees, etc. In other words, while multinationals were *exporting* capital worth $50 billion, they were *importing* income to the tune of $132 billion, while at the same time more than tripling their foreign holdings. As the *Wall Street Journal* once remarked (November 1, 1973), "U.S. corporations have created real money-making machines by investing in operations abroad." What was true in 1973 is more so today. The significance of this phenomenon for the economy as a whole and for the formation of U.S. foreign policy is greatly enhanced by two further facts: first, almost all the multinationals are among the 500 or so giant corporations which dominate the economy, and second, by far the most lucrative area of foreign investment is in the underdeveloped countries (in the 1966–1978 period the outflow of capital to these countries was only $11 billion, while the return flow of income was a fabulous $56 billion).*

Balance of Payments. Everyone who reads the financial pages of the newspapers these days knows that the U.S. balance of payments (i.e., the comparison of total inflows and outflows of funds on all accounts, private and public) is in plenty of trouble. Outflows consistently exceed inflows, and the dollars the United States ships out to make up the difference constitute in effect a debt owing to foreigners and at the same time swell the world's money supply, adding to already intolerable inflationary pressures. But how much worse the situation would be if it were not for the enormous inflows received from private foreign investments! Balance-of-payments statistics are notoriously tricky, and we will not attempt an accurate assessment of the overall importance of foreign investment income here. Suffice it to point out that for almost the entire period since the early 1950s, the persistent balance-of-payments deficits of the United States were created by the fact that U.S. expenditures abroad for military operations, foreign aid, and foreign investment were larger than the gains made by an excess of exports over imports of goods and services. But even the latter positive balance would have been a whopping deficit if not for the large and growing income from investments abroad. (Investment income is counted as payment for the services of U.S.-owned capital, in accordance with accepted bourgeois theory.) Thus, we find that for the period 1966–1978 there was a

---

*All figures in this paragraph are from the annual surveys of foreign investment of the Department of Commerce's *Survey of Current Business*, the latest of which is in the issue of August 1979.

cumulative surplus of $59.4 billion in the balance of goods and services. But if the flow of investment income were eliminated, this surplus would have turned into a *deficit* on goods and services of $152.7 billion.* It seems that not only the giant corporations but also the national economy as a whole has become crucially dependent on the income from foreign investment.

Foreign Involvement of Banks. During the last decade and a half a truly sensational explosion has taken place in the foreign operations of major U.S. banks. As can be seen in the accompanying table (page 166) a few figures tell the story. In 1960, eight U.S. banks had a total of 131 foreign branches with combined assets of $3.5 billion. By 1978 these figures had grown to 137 banks, 761 branches, and assets of $270 billion (increases respectively of 1,612 percent, 481 percent, and 7,614 percent). Furthermore, the share of foreign earnings in total earnings of the thirteen largest U.S. banks grew from 18.8 percent in 1970 to 49.6 in 1976, an increase of 164 percent in six years.† Nothing like this ever happened before in the history of banking in the United States or anywhere else. From being an essentially domestic institution the U.S. banking system almost overnight became international in the fullest sense of the term. In judging the significance of this international explosion of U.S. banking, one must keep in mind what has long been well known, that banks exercise great economic power; and what is only beginning to be well known, that their political power is commensurate with their economic power. Two featured stories in the *New York Times* in recent years symbolize this new awareness. The first (December 23, 1977) ran under the headline "Banks' Lobby Called Strongest in Capital," the second (March 18, 1979) under the headline "U.S. Banks Are Making Foreign Policy."

---

*These figures were calculated from data presented in the *Survey of Current Business,* June 1979. They are not strictly comparable to the preceeding figures on foreign investment: the inflow of income also includes, in addition to income on direct investment, income on other kinds of foreign investment.

†These percentages were calculated from data presented in the U.N. Commission on Transnational Corporations, *Transnational Corporations in World Development: A Re-Examination* (New York: United Nations Economic and Social Council, March 20, 1978), p. 218.

Table 15-2
The International Expansion of U.S. Banks

	Number of U.S. Banks with Foreign Branches	Number of Foreign Branches	Assets of Foreign Branches ($ billions)
1960	8	131	3.5
1965	13	211	9.1
1970	79	536	59.8
1978	137	761	270.0

Source: Board of Governors of the Federal Reserve System.

The relevance of all this to U.S. foreign policy should be obvious. In the period since the Second World War during which the United States occupied a dominant position in the global capitalist system, the U.S. economy developed a whole network of relations with foreign countries which became increasingly crucial to the operation, stability, and profitability of American business and finance. Under these circumstances one does not need to be a crude economic determinist to understand that what is perceived to be the national interest, not only by those who are the chief beneficiaries of the system but also by those whose livelihood is threatened by an interruption or breakdown in its functioning, is the preservation of the international status quo and, where this is not possible, to hold change within the narrowest possible limits. And indeed this has been the main thrust of U.S. foreign policy during every postwar administration from Truman to Carter.

It follows that in order to understand U.S. foreign policy in the period ahead, we must first identify the forces which threaten the status quo in ways likely to upset the stability and profitability of the U.S. economy.

As we have already seen, the answer is *not* the Soviet Union, which in fact has become an increasingly valuable customer for U.S. goods and a borrower of U.S. funds in recent years. There have been many changes unfavorable to U.S. capitalism since the Second World War. None has been initiated by the USSR—from China in 1949 to Iran in 1979. It is true that the Soviet Union has helped some (though not all) of these initiatives, but attempting to deal with them by striking at the Soviet Union (which was the central idea of John Foster Dulles's ill-fated doctrine of "massive retaliation") was never feasible and would always have been self-defeating.

The *source* of these changes—aside from what may have originated in the growing strength of America's advanced capitalist allies, which is an entirely different story—was in every case national liberation movements in the Third World, usually combining nationalistic and social revolutionary elements and in all cases carrying threats to U.S. economic and political interests in the countries affected. All signs are that these movements are active in various parts of the world today (Southern Africa, Central America, the Caribbean) and are likely to become so in others (South America, the Middle East, Southern Asia) in the not distant future. Deteriorating economic conditions and mass living standards in all but a few Third World countries (OPEC, South Korea, Taiwan, Hong Kong, Singapore) virtually guarantee that what may be called the revolt of the Third World will steadily grow in intensity during the 1980s.

This, and not superpower rivalry, is the number one contradiction in the world today and in the foreseeable future, hence also the primary concern of U.S. foreign policy.* How can Washington seek to deal with the problem? Barring a fundamental change in internal U.S. politics, which is hardly a near-term prospect, the answer has to be that the U.S. course will continue along the lines followed during the whole postwar period—supporting reactionary and oppressive regimes where at all possible, CIA subversion, and as a last resort military intervention.

This is where the alleged threat from the USSR comes in handy. As we have seen, it isn't the real problem, but to the extent

---

*This is not to say that somewhere along the road war with the Soviet Union may not break out. The U.S. budget for "defense" is geared to developing the capability of wiping out the Soviet Union in one blow. What we are arguing here is that underlying this rivalry and the accompanying arms race, from the standpoint of the United States and its allies, is the urgency to keep the status quo in what is left of the capitalist world, including, where possible, counter-revolutions in countries that have broken away from the imperialist system.

that it is believed to be, or that the public can be persuaded to believe it to be, the policies actually needed to combat the revolt of the Third World can be made politically palatable and even popular. While the people of this country might balk at sending U.S. forces to fight against national liberation movements in, say, Southern Africa or Central America, they would obviously feel quite differently if they could be convinced that the purpose was to keep from being crushed by the other superpower. So a policy aimed at defeating the revolt of the Third World will in all probability continue to be pursued in the name of combatting the Soviet Union. The clearest possible proof of this intent is the much publicized plan of the Carter administration to build up a 100,000-man rapid strike force capable of instant intervention anywhere in the world. Ostensibly its mission would be to counter possible Soviet thrusts, supposedly most likely in the present conjuncture in the Persian Gulf area. But the truth is that its only rational use would be to intervene to put down revolts against oppressive Third World regimes no longer able to defend themselves against their own people.

Three final questions: Can such anti-popular and counter-revolutionary wars of intervention really be won in the world of today? Or will they prove to be new Vietnams? And if the latter, how long will the American people continue to support them? We don't know the answers, but we are pretty sure these are the right questions.

16.
The Uses and Abuses of
Measuring Productivity

A year ago in this space we analyzed the spurious nature of the alarms over what has been happening to U.S. productivity (see Chapter 11 of this volume). Since then there has been no letup in the beating of the drums. It is now widely taken for granted, even within the ranks of labor, that productivity has in fact been declining and that this supposed decline is at the root of most of our economic ills. At the same time what is becoming increasingly clear is that the incessant propaganda around this question is being used to attack labor: to justify turning the clock back on conditions in the workplace.

Thus, the big stumbling block during the negotiations to settle the recent strike of New York City's subway and bus workers was not so much wages as management's insistence that the workers relinquish improvements in working conditions that had been won in previous contracts. These "givebacks"—for example, eliminating twenty-minute rest periods—were demanded by New York's Metropolitan Transportation Authority on the grounds that they were absolutely essential for the sake of raising productivity. While there is considerable doubt that the concessions ultimately made by the union will actually result in improved efficiency, the important thing from management's viewpoint is that the principle of givebacks has been established. This New York City development is far from an isolated phenomenon. Capital's demand for givebacks—to reverse labor's hard-won gains on working conditions—has been spreading from one in-

This article originally appeared in the June 1980 issue of *Monthly Review*.

dustry to another. And the groundwork for this shift in the class struggle has been laid in the so far successful brainwashing of the public to believe that the United States is in trouble because of sagging labor productivity.

The most remarkable aspect of all this hullabaloo about productivity is that it is based on absolutely phoney statistics, which, owing to their frequent repetition and prominent display in the press, are accepted as valid and meaningful measures. A striking example of how misleading and false these figures can be is provided by the construction industry. The official data, as computed by the government's statisticians, show that productivity in the construction industry rose over 70 percent from 1949 to 1967, and since then declined by over 20 percent. In other words, construction workers today presumably produce one fifth less in an hour than they did in 1967.

Experts in this industry, however, are becoming increasingly aware that these numbers have no relation to reality. (See "A Productivity Drop that Nobody Believes," *Business Week,* February 25, 1980.) In fact, field studies of changes in labor requirements for specific types of construction, conducted by the U.S. Labor Department, have revealed that productivity has indeed been rising during the same period that the index of productivity for the industry as a whole has reported a precipitous decline. What is the explanation of this statistical sleight-of-hand?

To appreciate the flaky basis of the overall productivity index, we must first recognize that the construction industry covers a wide range of activities: highways, office buildings, warehouses, shopping centers, factories, apartment buildings, one-family residences—these and many other types of construction are included under one rubric. Clearly, these diverse types of output cannot easily be summarized in one statistic. The method adopted by statisticians for handling this problem is therefore to add up the monetary value (usually the sales price) of each type of construction. The difficulty with this procedure is that the resulting numbers reflect not only changes in output but inflationary trends as well.

To get around this, government statisticians use a weighted average of construction wage rates and materials costs to deflate the dollar value of construction. But, as the *Business Week* article referred to above points out, "for decades, [this] standard solution to [the] problem [of arriving at a measure of the physical volume of all types of construction combined] has been a nonsolution." The reason is that it does not take into account the diversity of the construction industry and the changes in labor requirements that occur over time because of that diversity. Thus, in some periods road construction is especially important, while at other times factories, office buildings, or apartment houses may predominate. In addition, buildings differ greatly because they are designed to fit specific spaces and to meet special needs of buyers. Finally, there are changes from one time to another even in the more standard types of construction, such as private homes. For example, a greater percentage of single-family residences in recent years means more fireplaces, insulation, central air conditioning, and other improvements than in the past.

The point of all this is that the amount of labor required may differ from one year to the next not because of differences in the volume of construction or because of changes in labor productivity, but because of changes in what is being built. And since the official index of construction activity does not take the latter into account, the two series on construction output and employment are not comparable. It follows that the productivity index, since it divides output by employment, is a meaningless statistic.

Apart from this basic fallacy, mention should be made of a technical factor that further invalidates the productivity measure. There is strong reason to believe that the price and wage indexes used by the government statisticians exaggerate the increase in construction costs during the 1970s.* For all these reasons, the same *Business Week* article, summarizing the opinions of various industry experts, concludes that "the continuing collapse of construction productivity is a statistical phantom."

---

*The estimate of physical volume of construction, it will be recalled, is derived by dividing changes in the dollar value of construction by changes in a weighted average of wage rates and raw material prices. Thus, if the increase in the denominator is exaggerated, the resulting ratio—purportedly measuring output—will be understated. And if output is understated, so also will productivity be understated.

It is important to understand the full implication of calling the decline in construction productivity a "statistical phantom." Practically every declaration on economic matters in recent years—whether made by the President, government officials, business leaders, or pundits from the economics profession—has advanced policy proposals based on the assumption that the slowdown in the productivity of the private sector is an indisputable fact. But this "indisputable fact" rests heavily on the calculation that construction workers are now doing one fifth less work in an hour than they did in 1967: *about half of the much touted slowdown in overall productivity is due to this statistical phantom.* It follows that if the construction productivity statistics are full of holes, the whole argument about sluggish productivity growth becomes suspect. Moreover, if in truth construction productivity has been increasing, as Labor Department field studies of individual projects indicate, then at the very least there has been no decline whatever in overall productivity.

Even more important than the flakiness of the construction data, however, is the irrationality of the very idea that the productivity of the economy is subject to measurement and that the results are analytically meaningful. What we have here is a classic case of statistical fetishism—a fetishism that evolved when the concept of productivity was transformed from what was once a clearly defined technical term into the present amorphous catch-all. As originally conceived, labor-productivity measures were confined to the sphere of commodities. Thus, if in 1970 a worker produced on the average, say, forty pairs of men's shoes an hour and ten years later sixty pairs of the same type of shoes, it makes sense to say that the productivity of workers in men's shoe factories increased by 50 percent during the decade. What makes this a meaningful statement is that the end product is the same in both years. Clearly, if the product made in these factories had changed substantially—let us say, to producing wading boots instead of dress shoes—an index of change in output per worker would lose meaning. There would be no way to know whether the difference in the number of units produced per man-hour was due to the change in the product or to a change in the amount of labor required to produce a unit of the product. Thus, comparability of product is essential to the rational measurement of productivity.

Because of this, many technical problems arise, especially in a dynamic environment when styles and design change frequently. This is not the place to expand on the question: suffice it to say that it is often feasible to arrive at reasonable *estimates* of changes in productivity in industries where there is mass production of a fairly similar group of goods from year to year—as distinguished from industries that are devoted to custom-built items such as specialized machinery or the previously discussed construction field.

Productivity measures become further removed from reality when they are extended to a combination of industries, as for example in designing an index for manufacturing as a whole. Here there are two problems, closely related to those already discussed. First, the test of comparability has to be met. The only way to arrive at an unambiguous measure is to compare changes in the amount of labor required to produce the same basket of goods from one period to another. To the extent that there are changes in the basket of goods between the two periods, the productivity index loses relevance, since we have no way of knowing whether movements of the index are due to different labor requirements or to shifts in the composition of production.

Second, a method has to be selected by which quantities of different manufactured products can be added up. The labor force is not altogether homogeneous, owing to differences in skill, intensity of work, etc., but this does not prevent us from attaching a clear-cut meaning to the concept of total number of hours worked in a given period of time. The difficulty is that changes in hours worked have to be compared with an aggregate consisting of numbers of automobiles, yards of fabric, tons of steel, and so on—items which can't simply be added together to reach a meaningful total. The problem here is one with which statisticians have long been struggling, namely, how to construct a satisfactory index of production. And experience has shown that there is no ideal (or absolutely true) way to do so: several methods can be used, each giving different results and having a severely limited meaning. Under the circumstances the best approach is to ask at the outset why productivity is being measured, and to which questions answers are being sought. The more specific and restricted the questions, the more relevant the method of measurement of production and productivity can become. (For a fuller discussion of all this, see Harry Magdoff, "The Purpose and Method of Measuring Productivity," *Journal of the American Statistical Association,* June 1939; and Harry Magdoff et al., *Production, Employment, and Productivity in 59 Manufacturing Industries, 1919–36* [Philadelphia, Pa.: WPA National Research Project, May 1939], Part One, where it is shown that appropriate index number formulas for the measurement of productivity differ according to the purpose of the measurement. It is also demonstrated there that to answer certain types of productivity questions, hours worked or labor required per unit of production is the most meaningful common denominator for equating manufactured products.)

One reason for including this somewhat technical discussion is to drive home the point that there is no such thing as a straightforward or "true" measure of productivity. And if this is so even in the realm of commodities where a reasonable, if limited, meaning can be given to the concept, what can be said about the productivity of service workers? There are of course service jobs that consist of routine, repetitive operations—e.g., in typing pools—where productivity measures may have some meaning. But how would one go about measuring the productivity of a fireman, a short-order cook, a waiter, a receptionist in a lawyer's office? It is in the very nature of the case that in most services qualitative changes are intertwined with quantitative changes; hence there is no continuity in the "output" from one period to another with which changes in employment can be compared. Moreover, it is typical of many of the service areas that the "output" cannot be separated from the labor engaged in the performance of the service; for that reason too there is no sensible way of comparing changes in output and labor. In other words, the notion of a productivity measure for most service occupations is nonsensical and self-contradictory.

Unfortunately, such considerations of elementary logic have not prevented statisticians and economists from producing a whole array of productivity measures, applicable not only to the private economy (combining commodity-production and services) but in some cases to government as well, useful for ideological and policy-making purposes. And by dint of endless repetition and selective emphasis, these statistical phantoms (to use *Business Week's* apt expression) have attained the status of indisputable facts and have entered into the realm of scientific discourse. What is in reality nothing but a crude fetish has thus become one of the most potent weapons in capital's struggle against labor and in support of an increasingly irrational and destructive social system.

At the same time all this statistical flimflamming has effectively served to conceal the deeper implications of productivity changes in the recent history of capitalism. The truth is that it is the enormous and persistent growth of productivity in the factory and on the farm that has provided a sufficient surplus of goods to support the growth of an expanding and increasingly complex service economy. The smaller the proportion of the work force needed to produce commodities, the greater the potential for an increase of service activities. Some of the swelling surplus has gone into providing services that enable people to live better: for example, in education, health, and entertainment. But a very substantial part has gone to support the interests of business in the competitive struggle for profits. This is what has made possible the rapid growth of employment in such areas as retail trade; sales promotion; advertising; banking and other financial operations; speculation in stocks, commodities, and real estate; legal and accounting services; and so on and on. It follows that whatever interpretation one may choose to put upon overall productivity indexes, the very fact of the continued growth of this surplus and the service economy it sustains proves beyond a doubt that the productivity of labor in the commodity-producing areas has been growing by leaps and bounds throughout the modern history of capitalism. And if this very real increase in labor productivity shows up less and less in benefits for the mass of people, the reason is the growing irrationality and wastefulness of monopoly capitalism as it channels more and more labor into activities having to do with the making and spending of profits and less and less into useful pursuits that could serve the needs of the people.

A good illustration of how this process works is supplied by the automotive industry. In 1977 (the latest year for which we have comparable data) there were 727,000 production workers engaged in car production. In that very same year retail automotive dealers employed 1,115,000 people. (Both of these figures can be found in the *Statistical Abstract of the United States: 1979.*) Since some of the dealers were engaged in selling imports, let us conservatively estimate that only 900,000 workers were engaged in the selling and distributing of domestic cars—about 200,000 more than were needed to make the cars! It can be argued that the comparison is biased since a portion of the personnel employed by auto dealers is engaged in servicing cars. Granted, but on the other side we have not counted hundreds of thousands of others who are employed indirectly in the selling of cars: for example, there were 200,000 nonproduction employees in automotive production firms, a large portion of whom were engaged in serving dealers, conducting market research, and other types of sales promotion activities; there were over 100,000 employed in the wholesale auto trade; and the close to $1.5 billion spent on advertising autos and the roughly $90 billion extended in auto instalment loans absorbed a goodly number of service employees. What we see here is a characteristic of the shifting trends from commodity-production to service employment: profligacy on the sales, finance, and distribution side and relentless cost-cutting (via labor-saving and other economies) in the production operation.

A recent Op-Ed page article in the *New York Times* (April 9, 1980) by an auto assembly-line worker offers some insights into what goes on in the factory:

> I was working on a sub-assembly line in an auto-parts plant. We were expected to produce 330 fire-wall assemblies per hour—five and a half per minute. My job consisted of several motions: I put two pieces of metal in a press, then pushed buttons to close it and weld the metal together. One had to become as machine-like as possible, repeating each motion exactly. I could, and often did, do the job perfectly without looking. The only way to talk to me over the noise was to yell sentence fragments in my ear every few seconds when I briefly leaned away from the machine.
>
> Though inspection wasn't part of my job, I picked out and threw aside defective pieces—until one day the foreman poured a box of

the scrap I'd thrown aside into my bin and told me to use it. On another occasion, in a different auto plant, a foreman told me that he was getting in trouble for scrapping too many pieces—not that they weren't scrap, he realized.

With such a mania for cost-cutting, it is little wonder that in 1977 and 1978 combined (the last two years for which data are now available) close to 19 million domestic autos were recalled because of manufacturing defects. (For this reason alone motor-vehicle dealers need a large repair staff.) There are no statistics—it should come as no surprise—on the number of workers with severe mental and physical illnesses attributable to the pressures of the speed-up and other health-impairing features of the factory environment.

In general, the obsessive concentration on the productivity issue epitomizes the basic rationality (or rather irrationality) of capitalist economics. To have enough of a margin to protect assets and profits, and to defend their share of the market, capitalists must pay constant attention to cutting costs in the production process. This inevitably produces a fundamental contradiction between enterprise and social accounting. From the standpoint of the enterprise, measures undertaken to improve the safety and health of workers, to make more trustworthy products, and to prevent further deterioration of the environment are all additional cost burdens. From the social point of view, the central problem is not cutting costs or raising productivity, but how and where to allocate resources in order to eliminate poverty and to improve the quality of life on the job and at home.

17.
The Crisis of American Capitalism

The view that American capitalism is in a period of crisis is now all but universal, shared alike by observers of all political and ideological persuasions. The important question is therefore whether it is of a temporary cyclical nature—as, for example, the representatives of the administration in power maintain—or whether it is something deeper and more long-run, as an increasing number of unofficial analysts believe. If the former of these views were correct, we would not need to spend much time on the subject. After all, cyclical crises have characterized the history of capitalism for at least a hundred and fifty years, and most of them have not left any lasting effect. Or perhaps it would be more accurate to say that most of them have had a beneficial effect in that they have been the means whereby accumulated distortions and disequilibria have been corrected and the system has prepared itself for a new advance.

But not all earlier crises have been of that kind. And one in particular, which is still very fresh in the minds of people of my generation, was a horse of an entirely different color. I refer of course to the Great Depression of the 1930s which certainly did not set the stage for a renewed advance of capitalism. The system was still stuck in a quagmire of stagnation ten years after the onset of the crisis. What it did set the stage for was profound changes in some of the leading capitalist countries—the best examples being the New Deal in the United States and the fascist regime in Germany—and it also and more importantly set the

This is a reconstructed and revised version, based on notes, of a lecture given before various audiences in England and on the Continent during May 1980. It appeared in the October 1980 issue of *Monthly Review*.

stage for the Second World War which finally brought the Great Depression to an end and opened up a radically new phase of capitalist development.

I believe that the present crisis is of this second kind: not one which will eliminate distortions and correct disequilibria, leading to a new advance, but one which will drag on, with minor ups and downs, bringing in its train historical changes and transformations as momentous as those of the 1930s and 1940s.

Everyone who deals with this subject, regardless of whether he or she considers the present crisis to be of the temporary or long-run variety, has to have a theory to operate with. The theory may be explicit and thought-out, or it may be implicit and not even consciously recognized. It seems to me to be especially incumbent on those of us who believe the present crisis to be of the graver kind to indicate, at least in rough outline, what theory we are operating with.

My theory is of course Marxist in the sense of locating the dynamic of capitalist development in the process of capital accumulation. But it also draws upon or combines a line of thought which originated with Michal Kalecki and attained its most complete expression in the work of Josef Steindl, published in the early 1950s, *Maturity and Stagnation in American Capitalism* (recently re-issued in paperback by Monthly Review Press). A simpler version was presented in Paul Baran's and my book *Monopoly Capital*, begun in 1956 and published in 1966.

This theory is best described, I think, as an "overaccumulation" theory. It holds that under monopoly capitalism as it has developed in the advanced capitalist countries during the twentieth century there is a strong, persistent, and growing tendency for more surplus value to be produced than can find profitable investment outlets. Where this situation obtains, as some followers of Keynes like Alvin Hansen suggested as long ago as the 1930s, the result will be a decline—or slowdown in the rate of growth—of output and income, with rising unemployment and falling rates of utilization of productive capacity. And this situation in turn puts an added damper on investment and economic growth. I said that this set of tendencies is both persistent and growing in intensity. The reason is that the process of monopolization—what

Marx called the concentration and centralization of capital—is a continuing one which has characterized the history of capitalism throughout the present century and is still operating. We can sum up by saying: the more monopolistic the economy, the stronger the tendency to stagnation.

Let me digress for a moment to comment on the strange failure of Keynesian theory to make the connection between monopoly (including oligopoly and other forms of blocks to competition) and stagnation, in spite of the fact that the period of its emergence— in the early to mid-1930s—was also the period when orthodox economic theory was beginning to deal seriously with the problems of oligopoly and monopolistic competition. The trouble was that Keynesian theory was wholly on the macro level (dealing with the economy as a whole), while the new monopolistic theories remained wholly on the micro level (dealing with individual industries and firms). It was left to Kalecki to be the first to integrate the two. And of course it was Kalecki's lead that Steindl followed up.

To return to our main theme: if a monopoly capitalist economy tends toward stagnation—in the same sense that it always used to be assumed that a competitive capitalist economy tends toward full employment—then the problem to be explained is periods of sustained expansion and buoyancy. The problem, in other words, is *not* why we have sluggish growth and persistently high unemployment but the opposite: why we have long waves of prosperity with vigorous cyclical upswings and only mild cyclical downswings. Stagnation is the norm, good times the exception.

Looking at the recent history of capitalism from this point of view, we see that the problem to be explained is not the Great Depression of the 1930s, as orthodox economics has always thought, but rather the long wave of expansion and relative prosperity which has characterized most of the period since the Second World War.

What were the forces behind this unprecedented long wave of expansion? If I were undertaking to write the post-Second World War history of capitalism, this is the framework within which I would work. Naturally in a brief survey one can do no more than touch on some of the highlights.

(1) Underlying everything else was the emergence of the United States from the war as the unchallenged hegemonic power in the global capitalist system—and also for a considerable period among all the nations of the earth, noncapitalist as well as capitalist. In the interwar period, under the pressures of the Great Depression, capitalism had disintegrated into warring currency and trading blocs. Now it was re-united as it had been under British hegemony in the nineteenth century, with a new international monetary system and a greatly liberalized trading system. The dollar was established as the unit of universal money by the Bretton Woods agreements; and the IMF, the World Bank, and the GATT were created to facilitate the functioning of the new global system. All this set the stage for an enormous growth in world trade and capital movements.

(2) Rebuilding war-shattered and war-depleted economies gave a spur to capital accumulation, to which must be added the effects of the militarization of the United States as the new hegemonic power. It is no accident that the postwar recovery of both Germany and Japan really began with the Korean War.

(3) New technologies growing out of wartime developments— electronics, jet planes, etc.—opened up expanded investment outlets.

(4) Very important was the process that may be called "auto-mobilization." This had begun on a large scale in the United States during and after the First World War and in fact it was the backbone of the U.S. prosperity of the 1920s. It included not only the expansion of the automobile industry and closely related industries like oil, rubber, and glass, but also the building of roads and highways, the spread of population to suburbia, and the far-reaching relocation of economic activity in general. After a long interruption during the Great Depression and the war itself, the process resumed with great force after the war, enormously facilitated in the United States by the extremely favorable debt-liquidity situation of individuals and corporations at the end of the war. In Europe and also in the more advanced of the Third World countries, automobilization began in earnest only after the Second World War.

There were other factors as well, but the ones listed were

doubtless the most important. All were basic and powerful, but all were necessarily subject to a sort of law of diminishing returns. Or, put in other terms, the stimulus which they provided, individually and collectively, to the worldwide capital accumulation process was bound to diminish sooner or later. Just when this began to happen and in what order as between different countries and regions could be the subject of many debates. As far as the United States is concerned one could plausibly argue that a definite slowdown began in the late 1950s and early 1960s but was at least partly reversed by accelerated militarization under the Kennedy administration and then by the Vietnam war. At any rate by the 1970s, as the Vietnam war entered its last stage, the trend was already clear. The logical result was that the cyclical downturn of 1974–1975 was much sharper than any of its postwar predecessors and also more uniform and concentrated in its impact on the whole global capitalist system.

Here we must pause to notice that capitalism had inherited from the Great Depression a belief, given its clearest expression in Keynesian theory, that governments have the power, through fiscal and monetary policies, to regulate their economies and keep cyclical fluctuations within narrow limits. The prescription calls for tight money and balanced or overbalanced budgets in upswings, easy money and deficits in recessions. The implicit assumption was that the economy would operate around a full-employment trend line, that budgetary surpluses and deficits would cancel out, and that the result would be relatively steady secular expansion and price stability.

But what if the real problem is not cyclical ups and downs but rather permanent stagnation? This question was not asked and of course not discussed or debated either. The answer therefore only gradually began to emerge through the continued application of Keynesian policies to the situation of the 1960s and 1970s when the new period of stagnation was beginning to take shape. Gradually, budgetary deficits became the rule rather than the exception, and the private debt structure—especially mortgage and consumer instalment debt—grew more and more rapidly. Conventional theory taught that the consequence should have been a corresponding expansion of effective demand leading to full employment and the need for appropriate restrictive policies. But what happened in the increasingly noncompetitive conditions of the sixties and seventies was that much of the increase in monetary demand was dissipated in inflationary price increases rather than in expanded output. Hence the emergence, beginning with the downturn of 1974, of the previously unknown and unsuspected phenomenon of "stagflation"—stagnation *and* inflation. For this malady conventional theory had no explanation—since, as I pointed out previously, it had never integrated macro and micro theories—and of course no remedy.

The prognosis suggested by the analysis I have been presenting is obviously not cheerful. It is one of continuing stagflation (with some sort of trade-off operating between the two elements of the combination, deeper stagnation acting to moderate inflation, and moderating stagnation tending to produce an acceleration of inflation), punctuated by more or less severe crises and panics generated in the financial superstructure of the economy.

But it is not only a radical critique that gives rise to a gloomy prognosis. Establishment economists, though they have no theory to account for the predicament we are in, are becoming increasingly pessimistic about finding a way out. Illustrative of this trend of thought is an article in the March-April issue of *Challenge* magazine by Alan Greenspan, a conservative economist who was head of the Council of Economic Advisers in the Ford administration. Comparing the situation today with that of 1929, Greenspan notes the absence of excessive stock-market speculation but believes that the rapid run-up of housing prices in recent years could play a similar role today. This phenomenon—which incidentally had a small-scale counterpart in the Florida real estate boom of the 1920s—is related as both cause and effect to the enormous growth during the latest cyclical upswing of consumer debt, which Greenspan considers to be the weakest sector of the U.S. domestic economy. Government statistics show that the proportion of disposable personal income committed to debt service is at an historic peak of 28 percent. But this underrates the seriousness of the situation since a fifth of households are debt-free, which means that a very large number are devoting a third to a half of their incomes to interest and repayment of debt.

Under these circumstances a down-swing, unless checked in time, could lead to a cascade of bankruptcies and a catastrophic drop in effective demand.

To this dangerous domestic situation must be added, according to Greenspan, two international considerations of comparable gravity: (1) the huge and rapidly growing debt of non-oil-producing Third World countries owed for the most part to the multinational banks of the metropolitan centers. With no prospect in sight of a reversal of the factors which led to this Third World debt explosion, the problem can only get worse, threatening alike the solvency of scores of governments and many of the biggest banks of the capitalist world. (2) Related to the foregoing but of much wider scope—since the nations involved include developed capitalist countries, those with centrally planned economies, and even the OPEC countries themselves—is the Eurodollar problem. Here is the way Greenspan sees the danger and its likely outcome:

> If inflation in the United States should continue (relative to rates in Europe and Japan) to a point where a cumulative disaffection with the dollar as a store of purchasing power erupts into an attempt at a massive diversification [into other currencies], either the dollar will fall abruptly, or worse, central bank support will create inflationary excesses of the support currencies.
>
> A collapse in dollar exchange rates could create severe international financial uncertainty and retrenchment—and could trigger the bankruptcy scenario outlined above. . . .
>
> With the world's central banks standing ready to flood the world's economies with paper claims at the first sign of a problem, a full-fledged credit deflation reminiscent of the 1930s seems out of the question. The real threat to the Western industrial economies is the inflation which would be triggered by an attempt to fend off the kind of deflation we had in 1929–1932.
>
> The overriding mandate of the world's monetary authorities to prevent a credit deflation almost assures policy overkill at the first sign of credit stringency and falling prices. Deflation would be quickly aborted—to be followed shortly by accelerating inflation and economic stagnation. . . .
>
> Thus, in today's political and institutional environment, a replay of the Great Depression is the Great Malaise. It would not be a period of falling prices and double-digit unemployment, but rather

an economy racked with inflation, excessive unemployment (8 to 9 percent), falling productivity, and little hope for a more bene- volent future.

When he gets to the end of his story, however, Greenspan shrinks from drawing what some readers might consider to be logical conclusions. What he has been talking about, he tells us,

> is still a low-probability outcome. There is a remarkable resiliency in the basic capitalist institutions which support most Western societies. Extraordinary shocks are required to undermine them. While I do not want to appear the protagonist for Pollyanna, I trust that in a hundred years Black Friday [October 29, 1929] will *still* be regarded as the beginning of the greatest economic upheaval in modern history.

In the absence of further elaboration, a skeptic could be par- doned for wondering what alternative scenario could accommo- date the impressive array of facts which constitute the bulk of Mr. Greenspan's article.

Let me conclude with a few remarks about the cumulative impact of the economic developments we have been discussing on the mood and morale of the American political leadership.

First, you have to understand that U.S. hegemony in the global capitalist system—and indeed in the world as a whole—was by no means an unexpected outcome of the Second World War. By the end of the 1930s the American ruling class (if I may use that somewhat ill-defined expression) was badly demoralized. The New Deal under the leadership of Franklin D. Roosevelt had succeeded in defusing what could have become a serious threat to the capitalist system, but it was very far from restoring confidence in the future. With the coming of the war, however, this changed. It was quickly sensed that the United States would come out on top and that this would open the way to what Henry Luce called "the American Century." *All U.S. policies during the war were directed at planning for and realizing this perspective.* Above all, this would be the answer to the problems which the New Deal had not been able to solve in the thirties. At times American pronouncements, par- ticularly those of Cordell Hull, Roosevelt's long-time Secretary of

State and the chief architect of U.S. war aims, came close to spelling matters out in just these terms. As Gabriel Kolko wrote in his indispensable study *The Politics of War: The World and United States Foreign Policy, 1943–1945:*

> In May 1941 [i.e., six months before the United States entered the war] Hull publicly enunciated the "few and simple" "main principles" of American economic policy, principles that the United States did not essentially alter throughout the war. . . . "Extreme nationalism" could not be expressed in "excessive trade restrictions" after the war. "Non-discrimination in international commercial relations must be the rule," and "raw materials must be available to all nations without discrimination," including the careful limitation of commodity agreements affecting consumer nations, such as the United States. Lastly, in regard to the reconstruction of world finance, "The institutions and arrangements of international finance must be so set up that they lend aid to the essential enterprises and the continuous development of all countries, and permit the payment through processes of trade consonant with the welfare of all countries." (pp. 247–248)

And the following year, in July 1942, Hull explicitly included the missing ingredient in this prescription, the necessity for American hegemony. To quote Kolko again:

> The future required American leadership in the world economy, "the opposite of economic nationalism," or a new internationalism which many American allies feared was synonymous with American hegemony over the world economy. To the colonial nations Hull's often repeated words conveyed undertones of a new colonialism: "Through international investment, capital must be made available for the sound development of latent natural resources and productive capacity in relatively undeveloped areas." And the supreme role of the United States in this undertaking struck many allies as potentially damaging to their interests: "Leadership toward a new system of international relationships in trade and other economic affairs will devolve largely on the United States because of our great economic strength. We should assume this leadership, and the responsibility that goes with it, primarily for reasons of pure national self-interest." Exactly this realistic theme aroused anxiety among the allies. (pp. 250–251)

Regardless of these anxieties—experienced most acutely by Britain which understood very well that its own prewar system of imperial preferences was the chief target of American criticism— the United States stuck doggedly to its stated goals throughout the war period, using the enormous leverage over its allies' policies afforded by their desperate need for Lend-Lease aid. The main institutional bases of the new postwar international order were put in place at the Bretton Woods conference in 1944 when the end of the war was not yet in sight. And after their military defeat America's chief capitalist rivals, Germany and Japan, were duly integrated into the new structure. Only the Russians resisted, but their strength was so depleted by the end of the war that they could do little more than remain outside the system, adopting a passive attitude and leaving the initiative in global affairs to the United States.

These successes of the American ruling class in the international sphere had their counterpart at home. In order to carry through the reforms of the New Deal period Roosevelt needed a popular base combining workers, farmers, blacks, and ethnic minorities—classes and strata which had suffered most from the depression and which had the potential to form an independent political force moving more or less rapidly in an anticapitalist direction. In the new situation which emerged after the war, all the leaders of American capitalism, regardless of their other differences, saw in this legacy of the 1930s a serious threat, perhaps not immediate but certainly in the long run, to their power and privileges. They therefore combined to launch a vast and unprecedentedly ruthless campaign of political and ideological repression which has come down in history under the name of McCarthyism. This too succeeded: the trade unions were first purged and then co-opted; radical organizing was in effect criminalized; and intellectuals were either frightened into silence or won over, by bribes or flattery, to the service of the new empire.

By the mid-1950s, the new order seemed firmly established and to have found its fitting hero-symbol in the person of President/ General Dwight D. Eisenhower. The mass media duly saluted what the late C. Wright Mills ironically labeled the American

Celebration, and the intellectuals of the New Mandarinate triumphantly proclaimed the "end of ideology." The rulers of America surveyed the world and liked what they saw. Add that by then it had become an article of faith that Keynesian theory had given governments the power to control the business cycle—hence to prevent the recurrence of serious depressions—and you get an idea of the mood which permeated the U.S. ruling class as the decade of the 1950s wound down. The future looked secure; all the troubles of the preceding quarter century were gone and happily forgotten.

Now, after the passage of another quarter century, those troubles are back again, right where they left off in 1939. Stagnation, this time compounded by inflation. The world, allies and clients as well as enemies, apparently slipping out of control. There is not even the ability, promised by Keynesian theory, to manage the ups and downs of the business cycle. The American Century, it seems, is falling apart long before the halfway mark.

If we are to understand what is happening in the United States today, we have to try to gauge the impact of these shattering revelations on the state of mind of our rulers. From supreme self-confidence, they have been suddenly plunged into doubt and confusion, even panic. What went wrong? What can be done? Where do we go from here?

These are the questions, but quite literally no one who counts for anything in the United States today has any clear or coherent answers. Under the circumstances it was probably inevitable that there should be a sort of instinctive falling back on the seeming lessons of recent American history. And unfortunately—for us in this country as well as for the rest of the world—the chief of these lessons is that war and war preparations, whatever else may be thought of them, provide a quick fix for economic troubles. That has been the experience of all the wars of this century, most markedly of course in the case of the two world wars.* Under the

---

*The United States was slipping into a severe depression on the eve of the First World War. Unemployment stood at 8 percent of the labor force in 1914 and 9.7 percent in 1915, dropping to 1.4 percent in 1918. Similarly, the unemployment rate was respectively 19 and 17.2 percent in 1938 and 1939 at the end of the Great Depression, thereafter plunging to 1.2 percent in 1944. The Korean and Vietnam

circumstances it is not at all surprising that U.S. policies, both domestic and international, have been moving in an increasingly militaristic and bellicose direction in the last few years. To be sure, the defeat in Vietnam, ending an involvement which had never been popular and which, as it dragged on, aroused strong anti-war feelings in large sections of the American people, obliged the political leadership in Washington to soft-pedal interventionist foreign policies for a time. But in retrospect we can see that this was a tactical maneuver, not a change in basic strategy. As the memory of Vietnam faded, so also did the new look of U.S. policy. All of this long antedated the taking of the hostages in Iran and the Soviet invasion of Afghanistan. What those crises did was to reveal the real state of mind of America's political leadership, generating something close to a war psychosis in Washington by the spring of 1980 and definitely re-establishing cold war as the dominant mood of international life.

If the foregoing analysis is correct, we have to see this reversion to interventionism and cold war on the part of the United States not as a temporary aberration, but as the beginning of a new phase in the post-Second World War history of the United States and the world.

How long will this phase last? It might of course come to an end in a new world war—a very real possibility about which, however, there is not much that can be usefully said. Otherwise we must expect that it will last until one of two things happens: (1) Either conditions emerge favoring a new wave of capitalist expansion which could restore to the U.S. ruling class a reasonable sense of security and self-confidence. This too, as the history of capitalism shows, is a real possibility, though I see no signs of its happening in what Veblen used to call the visible future. (2) Or the United States learns to control its economy in ways that bourgeois ideology and social science have as yet not even been willing to contem-

---

wars show a similar pattern though in much milder form. The rate was 5.6 percent in 1949, the year before the outbreak of the Korean War, declining to 2.7 percent in 1953, the last year of fighting. Dating the Vietnam war is more difficult, but averages for the first and second halves of the decade of the sixties illustrate this point: for 1960–1964, the rate was 5.1 percent, and for 1965–1969 it was 3.4 percent.

plate, though this may change as the general crisis of the system drags on, and especially as the consequence of a particularly severe financial "crisis within the crisis" of the kind alluded to above. Socialists are of course convinced that a controlled economy producing for social need rather than private profit is feasible and would be in the best interests of the working people of the country, who constitute the great majority of its population. But the working people themselves are not now convinced of this, and whether or when they will be is quite unpredictable.

In the meantime those of us who understand the terrible dangers inherent in the new turn history has taken need not simply sit back and await disaster or deliverance. Perhaps most important at this stage is to gain time—time for the full seriousness of the situation to sink in, for passions to cool, for wise council to be voiced and heeded. To make this possible we urgently need to convince more and more Americans of all classes that the world has changed, that while in the past war brought economic prosperity, today even a non-nuclear war is more likely to exacerbate all the ills from which we already suffer—shortage of oil and other raw materials, inflation, unemployment, urban chaos. And we need to convince America's friends and allies abroad that they can best serve their own interest, as well as the interests of the rest of the world, by firmly refusing to cooperate in any way with new warlike adventures.

18.
Are Low Savings Ruining the U.S. Economy?

One of the strangest alibis for the diseases of the U.S. economy is that this country is sliding backward because the people have not been saving enough. Although this notion is so energetically and widely propagated that it has become an article of faith in economic and political discourse, it is based on a totally false analysis of capitalist investment behavior and on an equally false reading of the facts on savings and investment. The underlying assumption of this new myth is that capitalists have not been expanding and modernizing because they haven't had enough money to do so. From this it follows, first, that if only the people of this country would consume less and save more, capitalists would have the resources and the motivation to increase their investments; and, second, that with more investment new jobs would be created, productivity would rise, U.S. products would become more competitive in world trade, and—miracle of miracles!—inflation might even be overcome.

A succinct version of this diagnosis was recently formulated by Professor Lawrence R. Klein, the recipient of the 1980 Nobel Prize in economics: "We have lived high on the hog and failed to modernize our plant and equipment. We must go from being a high-consumption economy to being a high-saving economy if we are to reindustrialize and improve our standard of living." (Quoted in *Business Week*, July 30, 1980)

The standard factual backing for this thesis is the oft-repeated claim that the portion of consumer income going into savings has

---

This article originally appeared in the December 1980 issue of *Monthly Review*.

Table 18-1
Gross Savings of U.S. Corporations

	Undistributed Profits[a] (1)	Depreciation Reserves[b] (2)	Total Savings (1) + (2) (3)	Gross Domestic Corporate Product (4)	Savings as a Percent of Gross Domestic Corporate Product[c] (5)
		Annual Averages in Billions of Dollars			
1955–59	13.3	20.6	33.9	249.0	13.6%
1960–64	13.7	29.9	43.6	327.1	13.3
1965–69	22.9	44.6	67.5	486.0	13.9
1970–74	26.9	68.2	95.1	715.4	13.3
1975–79	59.2	109.3	168.5	1178.5	14.3

(a)   Profits after taxes and distribution of dividends. Profits from foreign affiliates are not included.

(b)   In the language of the national product accounts, this is the capital consumption allowance without capital consumption adjustment.

(c)   Column (3) as a percent of column (4).

Note: Columns (3) and (4) are not strictly comparable. The gross domestic product of corporations data are estimates based on adjustments of the statistics on profits and depreciation resreves to make them conform with the definition of gross national product. The resulting discrepancy, however, does not in our opinion invalidate the comparison for the purpose of showing that corporate savings have not been declining.

Source: U.S. Department of Commerce, *The National Income and Product Accounts of the United States, 1929–74, Statistical Tables* (Washington, D.C.: U.S. Government Printing Office, 1977) and *Survey of Current Business,* July issues, 1976–1980.

sharply declined during the past decade. The official statistics do indeed support this contention. For example, personal savings, as calculated by the Department of Commerce, decreased from 7.4 percent of disposable income (income after taxes) in 1970 to 4.5 percent in 1979. We will soon examine the validity of these data. But before doing so, it is necessary to point out that the much larger and more significant source of savings—that of corporations—is generally ignored in discussions of this subject. The reason for this neglect is not hard to understand, since in that area the available facts flatly contradict the cries of alarm about a precipitous decline in savings.

The relevant data on the course of corporate savings during the past twenty-five years are shown in Table 18-1. The first column of the table contains the estimates of undistributed profits derived from domestic operations of corporations.* These are the profits that remain in the corporation after payment of corporate income taxes and the distribution of dividends. (It is up to each company's board of directors to decide how much, if any, of the after-tax profits are distributed as dividends to owners of common stock. Undistributed profits as a source of savings for investment purposes could therefore have been larger if dividend payments had been lower.)

In addition to undistributed profits, corporations have another and even larger source of savings—the reserves set aside for depreciation, shown in column (2). In accounting theory these funds are supposed to be accumulated for the purpose of replacing plant and equipment worn out in the process of production. But in fact there is absolutely no reason to assume that funds accruing in the form of depreciation reserves will be used to duplicate the old machines and technology. Except in the case of irreparable breakdown, the need to scrap old productive capacity is rarely clear-cut.† The decision on whether to replace, and if so with what, depends on management's view of the profit advantages of the various options open to it. And due to the relentless progress of technology during the long life-span of installed equipment, what is available is generally very different from what was installed

---

*These figures would of course be considerably larger if the net income from foreign investments had been included. But for the sake of comparability with available data on gross corporate product, which cover only domestic operations, earnings in the form of dividends, branch profits, royalties, management fees, etc. from foreign operations are not covered in column (1).

†One of us had the opportunity during the Second World War to study the operations of machine-tool plants. The differences found in replacement policies of producers of similar machine tools was striking. For example, in a Midwest center of machine-tool makers one manufacturer had a firm policy of replacing his metal-working machinery every ten years. In another firm, located on the same street, the production manager prided himself on the efficiency of the over-thirty-year-old machinery in place.

in the past. Therefore, "pure" replacement rarely takes place: when depreciation reserves are used ostensibly for replacement they are, more often than not, invested in more advanced, more productive, and even enlarged capacity. Finally, there is no law that says depreciation reserves must be used to keep on manufacturing the same products. These funds are in effect savings that are available for whatever management thinks will yield the best profits: corporations in steel and other troubled industries are using these accumulating funds to spread out into other fields.

The two types of corporate savings (retained earnings and depreciation allowances) are added together in column (3). As might be expected, total gross savings rise at a rapid rate from one period to another. But that could be due to the larger volume of corporate activity or simply to inflation. The significant figures are therefore to be found in column (5), where savings are measured as a percent of total domestic corporate output (in current dollars) shown in column (4). The striking aspect of this measure is the approximate stability of corporate savings during the past twenty-five years. It should be noted that differences of half a percent or even a whole percent between one period and another are not necessarily significant in view of the margin of error involved in making these estimates.* But even if one wanted to make a point about the fluctuations shown for the last decade, it is noteworthy that two of the five years in the somewhat declining 1970–1974 period were recession years and that this was more than made up for by the rise in corporate savings to 14.3 percent of corporate output in the following period—a period that included the severe recession year of 1975. One thing is therefore crystal clear from the data summarized in Table 18-1: *there has been no erosion of corporate savings in the past twenty-five years.*

On the other hand, the criers of alarm do at first blush seem to

---

*The data shown in Table 18-1 are part of the national income and output accounts prepared by the Department of Commerce. They are estimates based on extensive calculations, in the process of which various assumptions and adjustments are made about incomplete and often defective underlying statistics. Because of this, previously published data are often revised as better information becomes available. In view of the size of these revisions, the differences shown in the last column (5) of Table 18-1 should not be taken too seriously.

Table 18-2
Personal Savings

	Personal Savings[a] (1)	Disposable Personal Income[b] (2)	Savings as a Percent of Disposable Personal Income (3)
	Annual Averages in Billions of Dollars		
1955–59	19.1	305.0	6.3%
1960–64	20.5	387.2	5.3
1965–69	35.5	549.1	6.5
1970–74	59.9	823.2	7.3
1975–79	72.6	1331.8	5.5

(a)   Personal savings = disposable income less personal consumption expenditures and interest paid by consumers to business.
(b)   Disposable personal income is personal income less personal tax and nontax payments to government.
Source: Same as Table 18-1.

have a case with respect to personal savings. The data consistently used by economists and the business press to demonstrate this point are summarized in Table 18-2. There we can see that savings are a relatively low percentage of personal income. Moreover, as column (3) shows, this percentage fluctuates from period to period. Seen in the perspective of a quarter of a century, these fluctuations are not particularly large and no clear trend is apparent. Nevertheless, what has set the alarm bells ringing has been a steady downward movement in each of the past five years: the average for 1975–1979 shown in Table 18-2 hides the fact that savings as a percentage of disposable income dropped year by year from 7.7 percent in 1975 to 4.5 percent in 1979.

But these numbers don't really mean what they seem to mean. We are here up against an instructive case of statistical fetishism. The measurement technicians long ago devised a set of definitions in which, for their convenience, the terms "personal income" and "personal savings" are used in a very special way, quite different from what you and we would ordinarily mean by these words. As a result, a limited, technical, statistical concept has become confused with the underlying reality. Let us explain.

For accounting purposes, the statisticians divide the recipients of national income into two basic categories: corporations and persons. The term "personal income" therefore means the income of all non-corporations: not only wage and salary earners, retirees, and self-employed professionals, but also noncorporate landlords, farmers, owners of unincorporated business firms, trust funds set up by the wealthy to escape taxes, nonprofit organizations (private schools, charitable foundations, nonprofit hospitals), etc. are included. The incomes of all these diverse categories are added up to get the measure of what is called "personal income." The estimate of "personal savings" is a residual figure obtained by deducting taxes, interest paid, and consumer expenditures from income.

Because of the statistical treatment devised to meet the needs of gross national product and national income accounting, neither personal income nor personal savings is a meaningful measure—if we want to know what has actually been happening to savings as the term is used in everyday parlance. Although this isn't the place to discuss all the technicalities, we do need to underscore two crucial points.

First, with respect to the personal-income side of the ledger, income derived from capital gains (e.g., from the sale of buildings, land, houses, corporate stocks, and other capital items) is not included. This is of course a very important source of income for the wealthier strata of the population. And although there may be justifiable technical reasons for omitting this category, its exclusion definitely depresses the official savings figures. Capital gains (from real estate deals in particular) have been unusually large and increasing in the years of rampant inflation, especially in the last few years when savings were supposed to be eroding.

Second, an even larger source of savings is left out of the official figures, namely, the depreciation reserves of unincorporated businesses. Because these funds don't fit into the definition of income, they are excluded from the personal-income statistics. And for the same reason they are omitted from the measurement of savings, which as noted above are derived as a residual from

Table 18-3
Increase in Individuals' Financial Assets

	Increase in Financial Assets of Individualsa (1)	Related Increase in Debtb (2)	Net Increase in Financial Assetsc (3)	Net Increase in Financial Assets as a Percentage of Disposable Incomed (4)
	—— Annual Averages in Billions of Dollars ——			
1955–59	31.2	8.4	22.8	7.5%
1960–64	42.5	12.3	30.2	7.8
1965–70	65.7	20.2	45.5	8.3
1970–74	120.3	33.2	87.1	10.6
1975–79	233.9	58.5	175.4	13.2

(a)   Includes currency, demand deposits, savings accounts, government and corporate securities, insurance and pension reserves, commercial paper, and miscellaneous financial assets.
(b)   Includes: 1. All instalment credit other than for the purchase of autos and mobile homes. 2. All other forms of consumer credit, such as credit cards at retailers, gasoline coporations, and commercial banks; check credit at commercial banks; etc. 3. Applicable non-consumer credit such as credit used to buy securities and loans on cash value of insurance policies. (The latter category also includes noncorporate business mortgage debt and some miscellaneous debt that couldn't be separated out.)
(c)   Column (1) minus column (2).
(d)   Column (3) as a percentage of the disposable income figures given in column (2) of Table 18-2.
Source: Calculated from data in *Economic Report of the President, January 1980* (Washington, D.C.: U.S. Government Printing Office, 1980).

income. In short, the official figures on savings grossly understate the real volume of savings, and in so doing render the year-to-year measurements unreliable.

Despite all the ballyhoo about declining savings of individuals (broadly defined), the simple fact is that their financial assets have been growing at a faster rate than income. This can be seen in Table 18-3 (the term "individual" used in this table is a misnomer, representing the same categories as "personal" in Table 18-2: individuals, noncorporate businesses, farms, personal trust funds, etc.). The first column shows the average annual increase in financial assets owned by "individuals": checking and savings accounts, government bonds, corporate stocks and bonds, reserve funds in insurance policies and pension accounts, and miscellaneous money-market instruments.

The increase in financial assets, however, is inflated because some of these assets were obtained with the use of credit. Therefore the gross figures on increase in financial assets are not a proper measure of the growth in savings. Unfortunately, debt statistics are not sufficiently detailed to permit a proper adjustment of the data in column (1). Information is available on the amount of instalment credit used to buy autos and mobile homes. As for the remaining forms of credit, there is no reliable way to know how much of it is used to buy goods and services and how much goes for the expansion of financial assets. Nevertheless, erring decisively on the conservative side, we have included in column (2): all forms of consumer credit other than that identified as being for the purchase of autos and mobile homes; and such relevant nonconsumer debt as loans to buy stocks and bonds and borrowing on the cash value of insurance policies. Since a considerable portion of consumer debt included here is used to buy goods and services, the numbers given in the second column greatly exaggerate the amount of debt used for the build-up of financial assets. Accordingly, the data on the net increase in financial assets, given in column (3) (total increase in financial assets minus the related debt) are very much understated. Then, for the sake of comparison, we present in the last column of Table 18-3 this understated growth in net financial assets as a percent of disposable personal income—the same standard measure used in Table 18-2.

The resulting picture is clearly the direct opposite of the much-touted erosion in savings. Instead of the fluctuations from period to period shown in Table 18-2, financial assets as a percent of disposable income have steadily increased. Moreover, the substantial rise during the past five years is especially noteworthy, since it is in marked contrast with the decline shown by the official savings data.

It is true that the data in Table 18-3, like those in the earlier tables, are not free of definitional and other technical statistical problems, which obviously cannot be examined in a brief article

Table 18-4
Nonresidential Fixed Investment

	Investment in Nonresidential Structures and Producers Durable Goods (1)	Gross National Product (2)	Investment as a Percent of Gross National Product (3)
	Annual Averages in Billions of Dollars		
1955–59	43.1	439.6	9.8%
1960–64	51.9	564.7	9.2
1965–69	84.6	808.3	10.5
1970–74	121.6	1187.3	10.2
1975–79	196.2	1925.4	10.2

Source: Same as Table 18-1.

of this kind. It seems to us clear, however, that they reflect a strong uptrend in financial assets and for this reason, at the very least, should make us deeply suspicious of the current wave of propaganda about the collapse of personal savings.

By now it should be evident that if there has been a shortfall in capital investment it could hardly have been due to a decline in savings. How could it have been if, as we have demonstrated, corporate and noncorporate savings have pretty clearly kept pace with the economy during the past quarter of a century, despite recurrent recessions and accelerating inflation? But, in addition to this, capital investment too has held up throughout these years, as can be seen from Table 18-4. The last column of this table tells the story: investment in capital goods as a percentage of gross national product has hovered around 10 percent throughout the covered period. This has been so even during the past five years when, according to orthodox wisdom, investment was being held back because savings were presumably shrinking.

Nevertheless, there are problems about capital investment— problems which have absolutely nothing to do with savings but everything to do with the nature of monopoly capitalism. This conclusion emerges when we investigate not where investment funds come from but the uses to which they are put. In this

Table 18-5
Purchases of Producers Durable Goods
(Billions of 1972 Dollars)

	1969	1974	1978
Rising Components			
Office, computing,			
and accounting machinery	3.9	6.5	8.9
Trucks, buses, and trailers	8.2	12.3	16.4
Autos	6.7	7.6	11.2
Instruments	3.1	5.6	6.8
Communication equipment	6.7	8.3	10.0
Total	28.6	40.3	53.3
Non-rising Components			
Machinery and equipment			
for manufacturing	18.1	21.2	17.2
Agricultural tractors and machinery	4.5	6.9	6.6
All other	19.6	20.7	19.4
Total	42.2	48.8	43.2
Grand Total	70.8	89.1	96.5

Source: U.S. Department of Commerce, *The National Income and Product Accounts, 1929–74, Statistical Tables* (Washington, D.C.: U.S. Government Printing Office, 1977) and *Survey of Current Business,* July 1977 and July 1979.

connection, the breakdown of investment in producers durable goods into rising and non-rising components, presented in Table 18-5, is extraordinarily revealing. A comparison is made there between three peak years of capital investment: 1969, 1974, and 1978.* The data are in 1972 dollars in order to eliminate the influence of differences in price movements among the various types of durable goods.

Although investment in producers durable goods has held up over the years, this was because of the strong growth of five types

---

*1978 is the latest year for which such data are currently available, since these estimates are undergoing another revision.

of such goods which more than made up for the laggard perform-ance of all other types of equipment. Thus, the rising components grew by 86 percent between 1969 and 1978 as compared with a mere 2 percent for all other types of capital goods. The non-rising components did show a somewhat larger increase between 1969 and 1974, but this group declined by 11 percent between 1974 and 1978.

What needs to be understood about the rising components is that they are in large measure related to the expansion of trade, finance, and other services. This can be inferred from the latest available information on the destination of capital goods, i.e., an input-output study for 1972. From that study we learn that trade and other services absorb some 60 percent or more of office, computing, and accounting machinery; autos; and instruments. (Autos referred to here and in Table 18-5 are only those bought by industry.) Trade and services even account for an impressive portion (36 percent) of the trucks, buses, and trailers category (the bulk of this type of producers goods of course goes to the transportation and construction industries). Communication equipment is almost entirely bought by telephone, radio, and TV enterprises.

Just as the rising sectors are largely influenced by the demand generated in trade and services, the non-rising sectors cater to the needs of the goods-producing industries: manufacturing, mining, and construction. And that is where the dog is buried.

What has been happening in these sectors is best seen in the case of manufacturing. Investment in manufacturing is sluggish for a very simple reason: the overhang of excess capacity from earlier overaccumulation. Thus, in 1979, prior to the onset of the current recession, manufacturing firms were operating at less than 86 percent of their capacity, according to the Federal Re-serve Board. Such a relatively low level of capacity utilization has been typical of all the peak production years during the past decade. Furthermore, capacity utilization has been falling sharply in the more recent recessions—to the low 70s in 1975 and 1980, levels which portend sharp drops in profits or actual losses. As an example, the severe decline in production and sales of autos during the current recession has resulted in unprecedented losses. This is all part and parcel of the general stagnation that emerged in the 1970s. And it is these interrelated developments—the stagnation tendency, excess capacity, and the fear of losses as recessions become more severe—that explain the snail's pace of investment in certain key areas. It surely has nothing to do with the availability of savings. For, as the figures show, where profit opportunities exist, investment funds have been available. And big corporations wishing to expand through mergers and acquisitions have not been deterred by lack of funds, nor have the wealthy who have been having a field day plunging into the rapidly growing speculative markets, such as commodities, stock options, foreign exchange, and betting on the future of interest rates.

What sense is there, then, in all the talk about reindustrialization and a shift from a high-consumption to a high-saving economy? Clearly, this kind of analysis serves the interests of capital in lobbying for government policies that will raise corporate profits, either through subsidies or tax cuts. And for reactionary politicians, it serves as a rationale for still further reductions in social welfare programs.

But serious bourgeois economists are also indulging in such diagnoses. This, as we see it, is a reflection of the bankruptcy of their theory in face of the impasse today's capitalism is up against. The truth is that a shift from consumption to saving would be self-defeating, since it would shrink the market for the products of investment goods (assuming that the savings would be used for additional investment). These days a genuine renewal of growth could be based only on a proper proportionate expansion of the demand for *both* consumer and producer goods. In the absence of some major new stimulus from outside the economy, this type of proportionate growth would have to originate in a substantial and sustained increase in consumer demand (including demand from the public sector for housing, mass transport, improving the environment, etc.). This in turn could happen only with a decisive redistribution of income from the rich to middle- and lower-income groups. But the obstacle to such a development is that the lopsidedness of income distribution is due to the structure of ownership of the means of production. As Marx wrote over a hundred years ago, "The real barrier of capitalist production is capital itself."

19.
Reagan and the Nemisis of Inflation

In an editorial published the day after Reagan defeated Carter, the *New York Times* (November 5, 1980) wrote:

> The voters understood all too well, we think, that neither man really knows what to do about the economy, the debilitating cycles of ever higher inflation and stagnation. Yet that is the issue, above all, to which the next administration must devote itself. Without a stable economy, there can be no significant social development or effective defense and diplomacy. And only sustained and extraordinary political leadership will produce a stable economy.
>
> On one crucial problem after another, a whole generation of leaders have now failed the nation. Once the confetti is swept up and the bunting packed away, it is the people's resentment of those failures that should haunt the nation's new leaders over the next four years.

The situation is even worse than the editors of the *Times* report. Not only does neither man know what to do about the economy: neither man nor any of their advisers nor the *Times'* editorial writer knows what causes the debilitating cycles they all complain about and rail against. They are all careful to protect themselves against learning what has become the nation's best-kept secret.

The reason for this self-enforced ignorance is not far to seek. Inflation and stagnation are not caused by inappropriate or misguided policies. They are inherent in, the outward manifestation of, the system of monopoly capitalism as it has evolved during the

This article originally appeared in the January 1981 issue of *Monthly Review*.

past century—the system of which the nation's political and economic leaders, emphatically including Messrs. Carter and Reagan and the owners and editors of the *New York Times,* are the main beneficiaries. If they were to allow themselves to understand this, they would be effectively incapacitated for the task of leadership, which is not to cure the nation's ills but to survive them while convincing the people that they are as much a part of the God-given order of nature as droughts and floods and earthquakes.

This is of course not to deny that some government policies make matters worse than others. The record of the Carter administration has been particularly dismal. Carter took office at the beginning of 1977 when the economy was well into a cyclical upswing which lasted until the current recession hit in the spring of 1980. Thus almost all of his term took place in an expanding phase of the business cycle. But the benefits of this expansion (GNP measured in constant 1972 prices grew by 12.1 percent between 1976 and the first half of 1980) were very unequally divided. The consumer price index (CPI) rose at an average annual rate of approximately 10 percent in the same period, which means that those on fixed or sluggishly rising incomes suffered severely. Even fully employed workers' earnings failed to keep pace with inflation (average weekly earnings rose 31 percent while the CPI went up 41 percent). Corporate profits after taxes, on the other hand, ran comfortably ahead of inflation, rising by no less than 54.6 percent between 1976 and the first half of 1980. (All data are from *Economic Indicators,* Council of Economic Advisers, October 1980.)

These few summary figures provide all the evidence anyone needs to explain Carter's electoral defeat. But is there any reason to assume that Reagan and Co. can do any better?

The answer of course is, absolutely none. The economic policies advocated by Reagan and his variegated crew of advisers do not add up to a coherent program which can be subjected to a reasoned analysis. But it is possible to say that the proposed policies that have a good chance of being implemented, especially tax cuts and increased military spending, would clearly add fuel to the inflationary fires; while those that would not, most notably balancing the budget through drastic cuts in nonmilitary spending, have virtually no chance of being implemented. This is not to discount the likelihood of a mean-spirited assault on the welfare system, particularly those parts of it which provide assistance to the most needy and hence least powerful sections of the population. It is only to state the obvious, that what could conceivably be saved in this way would hardly make a dent in the present budget deficit, let alone the much bigger deficits that tax cuts and increased military spending would entail.

What about monetary policy? Is there any chance that changes in this area could have a serious impact on inflation? One cannot completely rule out the possibility. There is no doubt that a policy of holding down the money supply, sufficiently ruthlessly applied, could check inflation. It would not directly affect prices, however, but rather would operate through jamming the brakes on the whole accelerating process of debt formation which has been crucial to buoying up the economy for years now, in other words by provoking a far-reaching financial crisis followed by a tidal wave of bankruptcies and debt liquidation. That used to be the mechanism through which inflationary and other structural distortions of the economy were eliminated, often at a fairly early stage of development. Throughout the nineteenth century and right up to the Second World War, such panics and deflationary debacles occurred roughly every ten years. But the experience of the Great Depression was so threatening that the U.S. ruling class came to the conclusion that panics were no longer an acceptable way of purging the economy of its recurring ills and fevers. After the war a new economic strategy was embraced. Its ostensible rationale was to manage the business cycle, but today after more than three decades of experience we can see that its real content was to prevent panics through institutionalizing and perpetuating inflation. The following data, taken from a remarkably perceptive article in the monthly *Morgan Guaranty Survey* (November 1980), tells the essential story.

This table is remarkable in that one does not even have to read the detailed figures to absorb its message: one has only to take in at a glance the distribution of minus signs and double-digit percentages. Through the 1940s recessions were marked by deflation, since the 1940s by *increasing* inflation.

Table 19-1
Prices and Wages in Recession Periods
(Percent Change at Annual Rate)

	Peak		Trough	Wholesale Prices	Consumer Prices	Manufacturing Wage Rates
Jan.	1920	July	1921	−29.4	− 5.8	− 1.9
May	1923	July	1924	− 5.2	0.6	0.8
Oct.	1926	Nov.	1927	− 2.9	− 1.4	0.0
Aug.	1929	Mar.	1933	−12.3	− 8.5	− 2.3
May	1937	June	1938	− 9.7	− 1.7	− 0.7
Feb.	1945	Oct.	1945	1.1	2.4	− 8.0
Nov.	1948	Oct.	1949	− 7.1	− 2.3	− 0.8
July	1953	May	1954	0.0	0.7	2.1
Aug.	1957	Apr.	1958	1.1	3.6	2.2
Apr.	1960	Feb.	1961	0.0	1.2	1.6
Dec.	1969	Nov.	1970	2.3	5.4	4.0
Nov.	1973	Mar.	1975	16.4	11.1	9.7
Jan.	1980	July	1980	12.0	11.7	11.0
Averages by period						
7 recessions, 1920–49				− 9.4	− 2.4	− 1.8
6 recessions, 1953–80				5.3	5.6	5.1

Reagan obviously has no ambition or intention to break this pattern and return to the *status quo ante*. Personally, indeed, he seems to be in tune with the wild-eyed "supply-siders" in his entourage (Kemp, Laffer, Winniski, et al.) who, consciously or unconsciously, are whooping it up for more rather than less inflation. Politically, on the other hand, Reagan is pretty sure to go along with the veteran wisemen among his advisers (Burns, Wriston, Rockefeller, Greenspan, and similar luminaries of the financial establishment) whose main concern is not to induce deflation but rather to contain inflation within reasonable bounds. This, of course, is nothing new: Carter and before him Ford and Nixon were also worried about inflation getting out of hand, and in the last couple of years it has been the chief preoccupation of the Federal Reserve under the chairmanship of Paul Volcker, himself a fully accredited elder of the financial establishment, whom Reagan, according to credible reports, may want to keep in that position. We shall return to the subject of deflation and depression presently; in the meantime, it is enough to note that in the realm of monetary policy what is to be expected from the Reagan administration is more of the same.

One thing, then, is reasonably certain, that inflation will continue in the period ahead and is a good deal more likely to get worse than better. One should not make the mistake of assuming that from the point of view of the ruling class this is altogether bad news. One need only go back and check the figures on what happened during the Carter years (see p. 206) to see why this should be so. Lower-income groups, including most workers, suffered not only relatively but absolutely, while the recipients of corporate profits were gaining both relatively and absolutely.*

Why then, it may be asked, should there be so much concern in ruling-class circles about the inflation problem? Why not just relax and enjoy it?

The reason, as we see it, is twofold. First, although inflation in the range of the recent past has clearly benefited the few at the expense of the many, it does not follow that *increasing* inflation would have the same effect. If walking inflation is good and trotting inflation is better, it does not follow that galloping inflation would be best. And the figures in Table 19-1 show beyond any doubt that the pace has been increasing for the last thirty

---

*Business propagandists insist that inflationary profits are to a considerable extent illusory. The reasoning is that depreciation which is deducted from income to arrive at a figure for net profits is sytematically understated because it is calculated on the original assets and hence will not cover the expense of actual replacement at higher inflation-caused prices. The fact is that even though this may be true for some industries, corporations as a whole have been making enough profits not only to expand dividend payments but also to accumulate capital. Thus, even in the decade of the most rampant inflation—a decade that also included a severe recession—the fixed capital stock (plant and equipment) grew substantially. Between 1970 and 1978 (the latest year for which data are available) the fixed capital stock of corporations (in constant prices) increased by one third. (Calculated from data in *Survey of Current Business*, April 1976 and August 1979.) In addition, while the business propagandists harp on the replacement-cost theme they ignore the other side of the story: inflation reduces the real burden of corporate debt which has been growing particularly rapidly in recent years.

years. So far, efforts to control it have been unavailing. If this continues, who knows what the future may hold in store? Our rulers are getting scared, and with very good reason. Second, and this may be even more important at this stage, the fact that inflation benefits the rich at the expense of the middle- and lower-income groups is increasingly obvious—and having increasingly obvious consequences. Ford's defeat in 1976 and Carter's in 1980 were both related to inflation. And it is rapidly getting to be a truism, even before Reagan's term begins, that if he fails in this respect as dismally as his predecessors the Republicans will be as unceremoniously thrown out in 1984. But this is not all. Up to now the mass of the people have reacted negatively to victimization by inflation—by staying away from the polls or by turning on the incumbent administration. From the point of view of the ruling class as a whole this is not all that important since it has firm control of both the major parties. But who can guarantee that at some stage, if things continue the way they are going now, the people will not conclude that it is the system itself and not those temporarily administering it that is the real enemy? It almost came to that in the 1930s. Next time, who knows?

So control of inflation, though *not* elimination of inflation, is a genuine issue, a burning issue, the most important issue apart from war and peace confronting the Reagan administration. What are its real options? How can we expect it to react in the limited time available to it?

Conventional wisdom says that since by now inflation is deeply rooted and feeds off the expectations it creates, the only remedy is a long period of tight money, slow growth, and high unemployment. Experience of course has already gone far to discredit this prescription: throughout the capitalist world money has been relatively tight, growth slow, and unemployment rising ever since 1974 without bringing inflation under control. But even if, contrary to all evidence, a continuation of the same policies through the 1980s could be counted on at long last to produce the desired results, it would be too late to save Reagan (and quite possibly the Republicans and Democrats too). It is pretty obvious by now that the conventional wisdom has lost its usefulness as an excuse for inaction and that something really different is going to have to be tried, at least in the United States, if government is to regain respect and legitimacy in the eyes of the people.

What can this "something different" be? Here we can appropriately quote what we wrote in this space ten months ago *(Monthly Review,* March 1980):

> The crux of the matter is that inflation cannot and will not be indefinitely ignored or tolerated to the accompaniment of pious declarations about wage-and-price guidelines, the need for monetary discipline, and the like. It will sooner or later have to be dealt with seriously, and there are only two possible ways: sharp depression or mandatory price-and-wage controls.

With the election looming in the near future, Carter obviously couldn't experiment with the deep-depression option even if he had been tempted to, which is unlikely. Had he chosen controls he might have won re-election, but he decided against and paid the price. The question now is how Reagan, with a full four-year term ahead of him and the ominous precedents of Ford and Carter behind him, will handle the inflation issue.

We noted above that Reagan certainly has no intention to provoke a severe depression, but this doesn't quite dispose of the problem. As we write in early December, interest rates are once again soaring into the stratosphere, and the economy seems on the verge of repeating the abrupt decline of last spring, thus following the course of what it has become fashionable to call a "double-dip" recession. The first drop was steep but also brief, tapering off by early summer, and the experts (if there really are any in matters of this sort) seem for the most part to agree that it will be much the same this time. But this is by no means a foregone conclusion. There are many weaknesses in the situation, especially in the area of consumer debt which we have had occasion to comment on many times in these pages, and an unexpected shock—say, a major bankruptcy or a dollar crisis—might touch off a chain reaction which could quickly threaten to get out of hand. Reagan would then be presented with a real opportunity, not of his own making, to put the deep-depression option to the test, following the example of Mrs. Thatcher's government in Britain. And there might well be some among his old-line, right-wing advisers who would push him in that direction.

On the whole, however, this does not seem a very plausible scenario. More likely, at the first sign of financial panic the concerned agencies of government, with the Federal Reserve in the lead, would spring into action with a variety of emergency programs (takeovers, forced mergers, bailouts, ready access to new credits, etc.) for most of which clear precedents have already been established in the last decade in the wake of bankruptcy or threatened bankruptcy of such giant corporations as Penn Central, Lockheed, Franklin National Bank, and Chrysler. Government intervention of this kind, forced on the administration in power by overwhelming pressure from the business community, would have inflationary rather than deflationary implications.

It is in just such a situation as this, it seems to us, that Reagan will be pushed, willy nilly, into adopting the only other anti-inflation strategy that makes any sense, i.e., price-and-wage controls. He is of course opposed on ideological grounds to controls, but so was Nixon. There are political imperatives that override ideological preferences. Nixon found this out and so, sooner or later, will Reagan. How much sooner or later will depend, we think, on the timing of the financial crisis which has been building up for years now and seems very likely to come to a head some time during Reagan's administration.

Looked at purely as a short-term anti-inflation program, Nixon's controls were reasonably successful. They were first applied in August 1971 and phased out the next year. This was during a period of cyclical upswing which ran from November 1970 to November 1973 when price increases would normally be expected to rise from one year to the next. As the following table shows, however, this pattern was clearly broken by the control program.

It is also clear from the table that the controls did not succeed in a way that some advocates had hoped. Reasoning on the assumption that a large part of the problem stems from the expectations of continued price increases to which prolonged inflation gives rise, these people argued that a break in the pattern would reduce expectations and in this way lastingly moderate inflationary pres-

Table 19-2
Percentage Increases in Consumer Prices
(1968–1973)

From August 1968 to August 1969	5.6
From August 1969 to August 1970	5.6
From August 1970 to August 1971	4.4
From August 1971 to August 1972	2.9
From August 1972 to August 1973	7.5

Note: August is used as the base month because the price-control program was begun in August 1971.
Source: U.S. Department of Commerce, *Business Statistics 1977.*

sure. On the face of it the Nixon experience tends rather to support those who argue that controls do not reduce inflationary pressure but simply contain it for a while, only to make matters worse when they are removed.

Neither of these arguments, it seems to us, gets to the heart of the matter. Expectations do of course play a role in the inflationary process but only because they have a basis in reality. If we are right that inflation is essentially only one manifestation of the way monopoly capitalism works, then inflationary expectations are an inherent part of the system and cannot be eliminated by *any* kind of temporary measures. What is required therefore is that *the way the system works* has to be changed. In other words the question is whether controls can be built into the system on a permanent basis and as a part of its normal mode of functioning.

The problem was never posed in this way in the Nixon period (nor in the various wartime experiences with controls), and very likely it will not be when the Reagan administration finally has to face up to it. But it will not go away, and the time will come when the beneficiaries of monopoly capitalism will have to choose between abandoning hope of bringing inflation under control, on the one hand, or seriously trying to change the way *their* system works, on the other.

In an interview in *Business Week* (December 15, 1980), the arch-reactionary, Nobel prize-winning economist Friedrich Hayek blurts out what many of his counterparts in this country may

think but prefer to keep to themselves. Expressing a strong pre-
ference for what we have called the deep-depression method of
combating inflation (for Britain, according to Hayek, the unemployment rate might have to go to 20 percent or more), Hayek is
asked whether he sees "dangers in continuing to fight inflation
with gradualist policies." His answer:

> Yes. That policy too easily leads to what the British call an incomes
> policy. Once you start that, it leads to a general price control system.
> What I most fear is that if the present attempts to stop inflation fail,
> governments will resort to price controls, and that would lead to a
> planned system for their economies.

So there you have the real alternatives: permanent, and no
doubt increasing, inflation; or deep, and no doubt recurring,
depression; or planned economy.

In a very real sense the first two have already been tried and
found wanting, which does not meant of course that one or both
may not be tried again. But somewhere down the road, we suspect,
the third is waiting for its turn. If and when it comes, it will not be
a "solution." In matters of this sort there are no solutions, only
battlegrounds on which groups and classes fight for their own
interests and their own conceptions of what society should be.
"Planned economy" is one such battleground, wholly new in this
country. The existing ruling class of substantial property-owners,
corporate and individual, which has had its way since the beginning, does not like the idea of shifting the battle to new terrain.
The dominated classes are as yet quite unprepared for the shift.
Which one will be able to accommodate to the new situation most
flexibly and to derive the greatest advantge from it remains to
be seen.

20.
Supply-Side Economics

"Supply-side economics" is a new name but what it stands for has been around for a long time. It is essentially a latter-day version of the doctrine given its classic formulation in what is known as Say's Law.* It holds that in an unfettered market economy, supply creates its own demand. In other words, if the system is allowed to work freely, production will generate incomes (wages, profit, and rent) which, when spent, will be just sufficient to clear the market of all the commodities produced. Two corollaries follow: (1) if there is unemployment and idle capacity, they can be automatically eliminated by an increase in production (supply); and hence (2) policy aimed at stimulating the economy need only be concerned with increasing production (or removing barriers to such an increase): everything else, including the demand for the resulting output, will take care of itself.†

If you believe this, and our supply-siders indeed do, the next step is to ask why the economy is in such as mess as it is in today. And the answer obviously is, because it is being prevented from

---

*J. B. Say (1767–1832) was a French follower and popularizer of Adam Smith. He didn't actually invent the "law," but he did popularize it.

†David Ricardo, the greatest of the English classical political economists, was a firm believer in Say's Law, to which he gave the following formulation in his *Principles of Political Economy*: "No man produces but with a view to consume or sell, and he never sells but with an intention to purchase some other commodity which may be useful to him, or which may contribute to future production. By producing then, he necessarily becomes either the consumer of his own goods, or the purchaser and consumer of the goods of some other person." Marx contemptuously dismissed this as "this childish babbling of a Say, but unworthy of Ricardo."

This article originally appeared in the March 1981 issue of *Monthly Review*.

operating normally, that is to say, in accordance with its inner laws. And what could be preventing it? Wrong-headed government policies of course.

Nor is it difficult for supply-siders to pinpoint the offending government policies. After all, what do producers (mostly big corporations nowadays) need in order to increase production? Plenty of money for one thing. And freedom from crippling rules and regulations for another. Hence the supply-side program: reduce taxes, especially on corporations and wealthy investors, and "get the government off the back of the private sector." The combined effect of these policies, so the argument runs, would be to "unleash the economy." Production would supposedly spurt upward; national income would expand in step; and, even with lower tax rates, government revenues would swell. With the return of full employment many government expenditures (like unemployment insurance and welfare payments) would decrease, and this together with increased revenues would produce the long-sought goal of a balanced budget. But this is not all: with productive capacity fully utilized and investment funds flowing freely, labor productivity would sharply rise, unit costs of production would fall, and producers would be able to lower prices without sacrificing profits. The crowning achievement of supply-side economics, consistently applied, is thus seen to be what the vast majority of the people want most—an end to the inflation nightmare.

The scenario is undoubtedly seductive, and probably won a lot of votes for Reagan. Moreover if its premise—Say's Law—were valid, it would stand a reasonable chance of being realized, at least in part. But the sad truth is that Say's Law is nonsense—childish babbling, in Marx's expression quoted above. There is no reason whatever to suppose that an increase in production, either by an individual capitalist or by capitalists as a whole, would generate either the right amount or the right composition of demand to clear the market. To most people, including especially businessmen, this is intuitively obvious. If they believed otherwise, they would increase production every time the economy showed a tendency to slow down, which they do not do now and never have done in the past. They wait until the demand for their products picks up—or gives unmistakable signs of picking up—before they increase production. The theoretical explanation of this behavior is not simple. In fact it encompasses the whole theory of the capitalist business cycle and obviously cannot be dealt with in the present context. But what *can* be said is that if Say's Law were valid, this kind of behavior would be totally irrational and there would be no such thing as the business cycle.

Here it may be useful to insert a brief digression on the history of Say's Law. Accepting it as an unexamined axiom, classical political economists (with a few exceptions like Malthus) had no theory to explain depressions (or "gluts" in the terminology of the period) and were forced to resort to *ad hoc* explanations—such as wars, bad harvests, etc.—of recurring hard times. By the late nineteenth century, however, the cyclical character of these fluctuations could no longer be ignored, and the neoclassical economists had a harder time of it. They too were wedded to Say's Law, and were therefore precluded from extending the main body of their theoretical system to encompass cycles of ups and downs. Their solution, if they bothered to concern themselves with the problem at all, tended to rely on the assumption of special non-economic forces acting on the economy in a cyclical way—e.g., the sun-spot theory of Jevons or Pigou's theory of psychological waves of optimism and pessimism. It was the great merit of Keynes to work his way through this thicket of accumulated confusion to a clear understanding of the absolute necessity to jettison Say's Law once and for all and to base his "general theory" on a more realistic analysis of the relation between aggregate supply and aggregate demand. This was more than half a century after Marx had clearly shown the way forward to anyone willing to pay attention, which obviously did not include any respectable economists. But after Keynes, Say's Law fell into disrepute and was dropped from what has come to be called "macroeconomics," i.e., the theory which deals with the functioning of the economic system as a whole.

Keynesianism as it is generally understood today, however, encompasses a great deal more than rejection of Say's Law. It also offers a set of policy prescriptions (fiscal and monetary) for dealing with disruptive economic fluctuations, which attracted a wide following among economists and in fact attained the status of a new orthodoxy.* To the extent that these policies were implemented by governments, which is itself a highly debatable subject, they failed to produce the utopia of a steadily advancing, crisis-free capitalism which was expected of them. As a result Keynesianism itself fell into disfavor. Its adherents dropped away in droves and began to search for something new and more saleable. It was under these circumstances that today's fashionable theories, "monetarism" and "supply-side economics," were born. Each is essentially a simple-minded revival of a long discredited theory—monetarism of the old quantity theory of money and supply-side economics of Say's Law. Both are in the literal sense atavisms, one of the dictionary definitions of which is "the recurrence, in a descendant, of a particular abnormality or disease manifested by a remote ancestor."

Let us now examine more closely the specific reasons why implementing the supply-side program is as nearly certain as such things can be to disappoint the hopes of its advocates. We can ignore the deregulation aspect since it is not the heart of the matter. This is not to deny that drastic lowering of environmental and worker-safety standards, clearly on the Reagan administration's agenda, may lead to some increase in investment in certain areas (e.g., in exploiting the natural resources of the public lands), but the amounts involved would at most be marginal. The real question is whether funneling tens of billions of dollars into the coffers of corporations and the pockets of wealthy investors is likely to generate an upsurge of investment and production. The answer is no, for at least the following two reasons.

---

*We speak of "Keynesianism as it is generally understood today" to indicate that there are significant differences between this general understanding and the ideas which Keynes himself set forth in his *General Theory of Employment, Interest, and Money* (1936). In addition to fiscal and monetary policies, Keynes believed that the preservation of capitalism, which of course he favored, would necessitate far-reaching reforms, including redistribution of income and extensive socialization of the capital investment process. Choosing to ignore this aspect of his thought, his latter-day followers have produced what Joan Robinson has called "bastard Keynesianism." Mrs. Robinson was of course one of the group of brilliant Cambridge economists who surrounded Keynes and helped to shape his ideas during the period of gestation of the *General Theory.*

First, the argument for the affirmative would gain at least *prima facie* plausibility if it could be shown that corporations are short of money to increase investment and production. But this is simply not the case. In 1978 *Business Week* reported on a survey of the cash position of corporations under the heading "Money Is There for the Capital Spending." A similar survey today would almost certainly yield similar results, only more so. Here is a summary of the findings:

> The nation's biggest corporations are sitting atop a record $80 billion pile of ready cash that could finance a grand boom in capital spending. . . . Instead the money is being fed out slowly, the pace of business investment remains sluggish, and top corporate executives and a good many economists concede that tax measures aimed at generating more cash as a way to stimulate investment probably would not do the trick. . . . [T]he relatively high rates of return available on cash invested in such short-term financial instruments as super-safe treasury bills, certificates of deposit, and commercial paper, coupled with all the uncertainties about investment in plant and equipment, make it all the more attractive to sit on money instead of spending it. . . . When corporations do spend today, it is frequently to retire debt, buy back outstanding shares, or make acquisitions for cash.

And in an editorial in the same issue (September 18, 1978) the editors of *Business Week* comment:

> The huge cash balances that corporations have accumulated in the last few years are a sign of something seriously wrong in the U.S. economy. In a period of healthy, sustained growth, this money would be going into capital spending programs to increase capacity and to upgrade the efficiency of existing plant. Instead, corporations are building up their bank accounts and short-term investments because they are afraid of what the future will bring and because they cannot find long-term investments that promise enough return to justify the risks involved.

We have analyzed what is seriously wrong in the U.S. economy in this space many times, and it is beyond the scope of the present essay to go over the same ground again. We need only underline what should be obvious to everyone, that stuffing the corporations with even more cash offers no hope at all of producing a remedy.

Second, some of the supply-siders argue that the problem is

more one of incentives than of money. Corporate executives are supposed to be discouraged from increasing investment and production by the high tax rate levied on corporate and personal incomes. A drastic cut in these punitive rates, they say, would touch off a surge of new productive activity. This is just plain silly. As J. K. Galbraith recently wrote in the business section of the *New York Times* (January 4, 1981), "No good conservative can hold that American business executives and their corporations are now engaged in mass malingering because of their taxes." And he might have added that if any of these highly paid executives were caught malingering, they would very quickly find themselves looking for new jobs. The problem of course is not activity versus inactivity but *what kind* of activity they engage in.* With industrial capacity only about 80 percent utilized (approximately the same figure, incidentally, as in 1929 just before the onset of the Great Depression), the incentive to busy themselves with expansion plans is naturally less than overwhelming. But it is precisely this situation which spurs them on to ever more vigorous and ingenious efforts to find other ways of fattening up the bottom line. They will naturally not only welcome but energetically lobby for tax cuts, but they are not about to let success go to their heads to the extent of installing a lot of additional excess capacity. There are, as the above quotations from *Business Week* indicate, lots of other ways to use the money.

The trouble with supply-side economics, to use a homely analogy, is that it operates on the principle of moving a string by pushing on one of the ends. The string stands for the economy: one end is labeled supply, the other demand. The supply-siders propose to move the whole piece ahead by pushing on the supply end. The result of course is not to move the string but to mess it up.

The analogy can serve a further pedagogical purpose. The

---

*In this connection it is interesting to note that much U.S. business literature is obsessed with the idea of "workoholism" among corporate executives, partly deploring its bad effects on their health, family relations, etc., and partly celebrating the intensity of the interest in and devotion to work that capitalism is capable of generating (often contrasted to the laxity and irresponsibility alleged to be characteristic of other social systems).

bastard Keynesian recipe for moving the string is to take hold of the demand end and pull it along. This makes more sense, and up to a point it works, as wartime experiences have frequently demonstrated. But if the string is pulled too hard and too long, it breaks at various weak points, and repairs cannot be made from either the supply or the demand ends. This seems to be about the situation we are in now, after a long period of capitalist prosperity stretching from the end of the Second World War to the early 1970s. For roughly half of this period, through the 1950s, the string resembled a snake, generating its own forward motion. But as this internal motive force petered out, more and more reliance had to be placed on Keynesian policies of pulling on the demand end (explosion of private debt and continuous government deficits). This, however, proved to be no panacea, as inflation speeded up and domestic and international monetary and financial disorders multiplied, creating a condition of chronic crisis.

Let us leave the string analogy there: further complicating it would do more to confuse than clarify the issues. It will have served a purpose if it helps us to understand that supply-side economics, to the extent that it is more than a cynical fig-leaf to cover a policy of redistributing income and wealth in favor of the rich at the expense of the poor, is a manifestation of the total intellectual bankruptcy of the U.S. ruling class.

Selected Modern Reader Paperbacks